Wellcome to Hell: Was Sir Henry Wellcome Jack the Ripper?

JOSEPH BUSA

WELLCOME TO HELL

Copyright © 2015 Joseph Busa

All rights reserved.

ISBN-13:978-1508550815
ISBN- 10:1508550816

WELLCOME TO HELL

WELLCOME TO HELL

To Michelle: for the good times ahead

WELLCOME TO HELL

CONTENTS

	Introduction	1
1	Hidden in Plain Sight	5
2	London in the 1880s	8
3	Serial Killers - Childhood	17
4	Early Life of Henry Wellcome	19
5	Sadistic Serial Killers – Into Dreamland	27
6	Burroughs Wellcome & Company	31
7	1885 – Freemasonry and the Ripper	41
8	1888 – Tipping Point	51
9	Martha Tabram – A Fumble in the Dark	56
10	The Police – A Slow Start	65
11	Mary Ann Nichols – The Makings of a Surgeon	72
12	The Press – Before the Ripper	79
13	Business as Usual	81
14	Annie Chapman – Another Curio for the Collection	83
15	Loss of Faith and the Creation of the Whitechapel Vigilance Committee	91

16	The Ripper Letters	99
17	The Double Event	104
18	A Legend is Born	125
19	The Blame Game	131
20	Mary Jane Kelly – A Tart Without a Heart	136
21	The End of the Carnage	145
22	He Snatched Defeat out of the Jaws of Victory	152
23	Alice McKenzie – One Last Hurrah	157
24	The Rise and Rise of Henry Wellcome	162
25	Marriage, Travel, Sex and Curios	165
26	Separation and Divorce	172
27	Honours and his Legacy	176
	Epilogue	178
	Appendix – The Usual Suspects	180
	Bibliography	199

JOSEPH BUSA

INTRODUCTION

Many books have been written about the identity of 'Jack the Ripper', the world's most infamous serial killer. However, one name is conspicuous by its absence, Sir Henry Wellcome, co-founder of the pharmaceutical company Borroughs Wellcome and Company, founder of the Wellcome Trust, Freemason and latter-day Pillar of the Establishment. The reason for this is unclear, as upon brief inspection of his life it is apparent that he should be included as one of the suspects for the series of shocking murders committed in the autumn of 1888. My aim in this book is to explain how I reached this conclusion, drawing a parallel between the upbringing and attributes of Sir Henry Wellcome and those of a serial killer.

The life of Sir Henry Wellcome is well known to some in the pharmaceutical industry. He was born in the backwoods of the American Midwest, studied pharmacy and went into a business partnership with Silas Manville Burroughs, patenting, producing and selling tabloids (compressed medicines) to the world. Together the two men established their world famous company 'Burroughs Wellcome & Co' in London in 1880. Over the years the original pharmaceutical company was renamed, with Burroughs' name being lost in the sands of time. The current pharmaceutical conglomerate is called Wellcome PLC and so still bears Sir Henry's name. Prior to his death, Sir Henry also established the Wellcome Trust as his lasting legacy to the world, the trust describing itself as being a global charitable foundation dedicated to achieving improvements in human and animal health.

Those that know of Wellcome's background will know that he was obsessed with collecting artefacts and books relating to the history of medicine. However, it appears less well known that many of these artefacts are medical tools that included surgical knives, weapons, suits of armour, death masks and implements of torture. Wellcome spent years of his life and huge sums of money building a massive collection of 'medical' artefacts, numbering well over a million items. The collection was so large that many of the items were to remain in their packing cases, never to see the light of day, with only a handful being used to create his Historical Medical Museum, established in 1913.

Opportunely, because Sir Henry Wellcome is such a famous man, his life has been documented, from his birth in America's Midwest right through until his death in England in 1936. Therefore, enough material is available to make a judgement as to whether this highly successful man, one of the driving forces behind the modern pharmaceutical industry, could also have been the world's most notorious serial killer. Despite all the good that Sir Henry's companies have brought to this world, I believe that there is a case for believing he was Jack the Ripper, one of the most iniquitous of men.

I have used this book to take what is known and rumoured to be known about Sir Henry Wellcome and linked the facets of his life to the attributes of the serial killer. I seek to open a window into understanding how the events in his life leading up until 1888 may have prepared the way for his becoming the Whitechapel murderer. I have included a summary of Sir Henry Wellcome's life; descriptions of the events that took place on the night of each of the Whitechapel murders; a summary of the existing prime suspects and finally an invitation to you to go and see an exhibition that in my opinion could give you an insight into the mind of the world's most famous murderer.

WELLCOME TO HELL

Please bear the following quotation in mind when reading through the remainder of this book.

A Native American elder once described his own inner struggles in this manner: Inside of me there are two dogs. One of the dogs is mean and evil. The other dog is good. The mean dog fights the good dog all the time. When asked which dog wins, he reflected for a moment and replied, the one I feed the most.

www.goodreads.com/author/show/5217.George_Bernard_Shaw

JOSEPH BUSA

CHAPTER ONE

Hidden in Plain Sight

In April 2012 I visited the Wellcome Trust's 'Brains: The mind as matter' exhibition held at the Trust's grand building on London's Euston Road. I went to see the exhibition because amongst the exhibits was a slice of the brain of possibly the most intelligent man to have walked the earth, Albert Einstein. Needless to say, it did not take me long to see the exhibit I was interested in, so I took a quick walk around the rest of the exhibition and then made my way to the coffee shop. After a coffee and a cake I noticed a sign advertising another, permanent exhibition entitled 'Medicine Man' on the building's first floor. The exhibition was free, so I decided to give it a look. I made my way upstairs and walked into a medium sized, wood panelled exhibition room containing a small selection of artefacts that had been collected over many years by the Wellcome Trust's founder, Sir Henry Wellcome, for his Historical Medical Museum. There were number of interesting exhibits, including Napoleon's toothbrush and a lock of George III's hair. Whether by design or pure accident, most of the items on display can be summarised as belonging to the following categories: Surgery, Sex, Death and Torture; I actually found the display quite disturbing.

My attention was then drawn to a painting named 'The Tooth Drawer', by the artist Luciano Nezzo. The painting depicts a well-dressed woman about to undergo dental surgery at the hands of a shabbily dressed dentist. The dentist is seen holding onto the lady's jaw with his left hand whilst hidden behind his back he is holding some form of gruesome tooth-removing implement in his right hand. To my untrained eye, the painting looks very much like a shabbily dressed man in the process of mounting a physical attack on a defenceless woman. I was immediately struck by the following thought; what sort of person would buy a painting like this? Looking around the room, I then noticed a cabinet containing surgical implements (including two 10-inch surgeon's knives) and another cabinet containing an anatomical model of a woman with some of her body parts removed (including one of the breasts which way laid out next to the body). Then it hit me, could this be a collection not of a medicine man, but of some psychologically disturbed individual?

I looked again at Nezzo's painting and imagined the scene, if instead of holding the dental implement; the shabbily dressed man was painted holding a 10-inch surgical knife behind his back. Then I wondered if the painting's owner might have held a similar image in his mind's eye. I can't explain why, but then it hit me, could the owner of this collection of grisly objects be Jack the Ripper!

I knew a little about the Whitechapel murders and thought I remembered them taking place in 1888. With that in mind, I took another look at exhibits and the descriptions about the man that owned them, looking for anything that might link Sir Henry Wellcome with the nineteenth century serial killer. I discovered that Sir Henry was born on 21 August 1853, making him 35 years old in 1888. I could find no mention of his being married and I was not even sure that he was based in London at the time of the Ripper murders. But what I did know was that in 1888 Sir Henry Wellcome was a single white American male, aged between 20 and 40 years of age and had a proven interest in surgery and death. My interest was piqued, so I decided then and there to learn more about both the life of Sir Henry Wellcome and the Whitechapel murders, to see if it was possible that, by a chance in a million, I had stumbled across the notorious Victorian killer of women, Jack the Ripper.

The names, dates and events recorded in this book are factual. However, descriptions of Sir Henry Wellcome's mindset, involvement in the murders and any involvement that he might have had in writing the notorious Jack the Ripper letters are a fiction the I created to account for how he might have felt and acted if he truly were the infamous Whitechapel murderer.

In writing this book my research has been based solely upon a few books written about this great man and his family, and from numerous books written about the Jack the Ripper murders. I have not seen any of Sir Henry's private correspondence or other materials held by the Wellcome Trust. Such weaknesses aside, I hope that I have been able to achieve my primary goal of shining a light on a man who up until now has remained invisible to Ripperologists and the millions of ordinary people who have expressed a passing interest in knowing the identity of the Ripper.

I believe that I have identified the right man and that it is now only be a matter of time before the final pieces of the jigsaw are found and the case of the Whitechapel murders are finally closed forever.

CHAPTER TWO

London in the 1880s

No book about the Whitechapel murders would be complete without some mention of the history of London, the capital city of the world's leading nation back in 1888. The city's history adds context to the life and times of its citizens, helping to explain the polarities between the lives of the elites and the destitute. Thus, setting the scene for the Whitechapel murders and providing a framework that helps explain why the police struggled in their efforts to apprehend the murderer.

In the nineteenth century the United Kingdom ruled the waves and the world. England was the richest country in the world and in London lived most of its richest citizens. Yet for all these riches, in the 1880s there existed a massive class divide, with many people forced to live hand to mouth. Thousands of people lived in what were known as the rookeries; slum areas where houses were occupied by so many people, that they resembled Rooks nesting in a tree. As Thomas Hobbes alluded to in his Leviathan of 1651, life for these people was truly 'solitary, poor, nasty, brutish and short'.

The slum housing of London is thought to have developed during the reign of King Henry VIII. King Henry's arguments with the Catholic Church culminated in the Dissolution of the Monasteries in 1539. Until then the monks had provided the poor with education and charity. The seizure of the Church's assets resulted in London being flooded with people from the countryside seeking work. The resultant increase in London's population led to overcrowding and the rapid expansion of multi-occupancy dwellings. In an effort to control the overcrowding, the authorities did something that was to have the reverse effect. In 1580 Queen Elizabeth I issued a proclamation making it illegal to build new buildings in London. It was no doubt hoped that this would stem the tide of people intent on making their way to live in the city. However, the poor had nowhere else to go and so continued to arrive in the city in ever-greater numbers. The only difference caused by the Queen's proclamation was that the newcomers had fewer buildings in which to live, leading to even greater overcrowding.

Over the decades, living conditions slowly deteriorated and by the 1660s they were ideal for the spread of the plague and other deadly diseases. When the plague finally arrived in London in the year 1665 it killed more than 100,000 Londoners. The city's slum areas were finally swept away a year later in the Great Fire of 1666. Up to 80,000 of London's poor were evacuated from the city following the fire. Most of the city was rebuilt following the fire but few of the poor had enough money to return to it.

The area of London of interest to our story is the land in and around Spitalfields located in the borough of Whitechapel. In 1666, the Spital Field was just that, a field to the east of London. Over time it would be subsumed into the city by the effects of urban sprawl and would become known as the now familiar Spitalfields. Building work started in earnest from the 1670s, when permission was sought from the Privy Council to build along the Southern edge of the Spital Field. Local people were keen for the area to be developed, as it was at that time being inhabited by "noysome and offensive people". No doubt some of the city's refugees must have relocated into the area, with their descendants no doubt going on to become the rookery dwellers of the 1880s.

Life in the late eighteenth and early nineteenth centuries had not been too bad for the Whitechapel poor. There were jobs to be had in the booming silk weaving industry, local markets and the London docks. The area's original occupants were skilled weavers from Holland, who had relocated to England in the early seventeenth century. Good livings could be made and times were good for the immigrant community of Spitalfields. The richest, built large houses that served both as homes and workplaces, with large windows installed to enable the weaving of silk by natural light. As with any thriving area, word spread of the easy life to be had in London and more people flooded into Whitechapel seeking employment. In addition to the natural tendency for Britain's indigenous people to be attracted to the city, large numbers of immigrants from other countries were to follow the Dutch. In 1685, King Louis XIV of France reintroduced the persecution of Protestants, with his revocation of the Edict of Nantes. This made France a dangerous place to live for non-Catholics and resulted in Protestant Huguenot weavers fleeing the country. Many would have heard of the good livings to be made in London's Whitechapel and then migrated there. Times must have been good, as the Dutch weavers welcomed the French Huguenots with open arms and even raised a massive public collection of £40,000 to act as poor relief for them. The good times were to continue for both communities up until the 1750s, with Whitechapel reaching its height of prosperity during the 1740s.

Then in the 1760s, life started to get a lot harder for the silk weavers, especially the lower skilled journeymen weavers, their wages were being eroded and they began to demonstrate for higher pay. In some instances groups of weavers broke into the homes of their employers, destroying their looms and stocks of silk goods. The Government of the day responded to these acts of aggression by introducing a law, making it punishable by death for anyone caught breaking into any house or shop with the intention of damaging or destroying silk goods. Fortunately, Government officials understood that the journeymen weavers' wages were being undercut by the oversupply of labour caused by the mass of people seeking work in the area. So in 1773, it passed the Spitalfield Acts, which restricted the supply of labour and required independent local Justices of the Peace to set wage levels. Times were now much harder than the golden age of the 1740s, but these acts appear to have had the desired effect of quelling civil unrest.

Over time, a combination of the invention of steam looms, foreign competition and too many unskilled workers seeking fewer and fewer jobs resulted in plummeting prices of silk goods. A final devastating setback occurred in 1826, when in the spirit of free trade the Government allowed French silk to be sold in the British marketplace. A 30% tariff was imposed on the imported goods in an effort to protect the indigenous industry, but this was not enough to stop most of the rest of the Whitechapel's master weavers selling-up and moving on to pastures new. Their once grand houses were bought by slum landlords and would soon fall into disrepair. Unlike the master weavers, the unskilled workers could not afford to leave Whitechapel and were forced to live in slum housing, trying to scratch a living from what little work remained in the area.

Things went from bad to worse in the 1830s, when in 1834 the Government revised the Poor Law. This new system seriously curtailed aid to the poor, greatly reducing the amount of outdoor relief made available to them. A degrading mandatory 'workhouse test' was then established, which resulted in the much desired reduction in numbers seeking parish assistance, but came at the cost of many of the dispossessed having to find any means (mainly illegal) in which to maintain a living. In 1845, just when many of Whitechapel's poorest felt that they had reached the bottom of the abyss, the Irish Potato Famine struck. This forced millions of starving people to flee the Emerald Isle, in the hope of creating new lives for themselves in foreign lands. Many Irish people made their way to an already poor and overcrowded Whitechapel. The result of the plummeting price of silk and additional immigration into the city meant that the decades between the 1830s and 1880s (covering the first 50 years of Queen Victoria's reign) were thought to be the harshest in the entire history of London's poor.

At the time, the main source of work for men was to be found in the London docks with tasks like the loading and unloading of cargo. You would have thought that the regular work that this required would have created many permanent jobs, but this was not the case. The unskilled dockworkers instead had to make their way to the docks each day to join massive queues of men hoping to get a day's work. Men were selected from the masses using a humiliating process called the 'Call-On' which consisted of the dock owners and/or their underlings walking along the rows of desperate men and selecting those that looked best able to meet the needs of the physically demanding work of the loading and unloading of ships' cargoes. Pay and conditions would eventually improve for the dockworkers, these improvements achieved in part by the growth of the Trade's Union movement, worker strikes and worker agitation. The first major success in workers' pay and conditions was to come from the Great Dock Strike of 1889.

However, before such heady days, a fourth wave of immigrants were to find their way to Whitechapel, arriving there in the early 1880s. Many thousands of Jews were forced to flee Russia and Eastern Europe in response to the pogroms that followed the assassination of Tsar Alexander II of Russia. The inhabitants of Whitechapel did their best to accommodate the new arrivals, but tensions were much higher than in the past, as jobs were scarcer and living standards lower.

London is unusual in having two police forces. The City of London Police are responsible for policing within the boundaries of the original City of London and the Metropolitan Police has jurisdiction for all the rest of the City. The Met was founded by Sir Robert Peel in 1829 and in 1888 was under direct responsibility of the Home Secretary of the day, Sir Henry Matthews. The system of policing worked well, but there must have been obvious complications in investigating crimes committed across the boundaries that separated the two police forces.

The late 1880's were known as a period of high unemployment and civil unrest. 1886 saw violent demonstrations by the unemployed in and around London's Trafalgar Square. The British Monarch, Queen Victoria, expressed her displeasure at the authorities' inability to maintain law and order. Her intervention resulted in the then Commissioner of the Metropolitan Police, Sir Edmund Henderson, resigning and being replaced by a military general, Charles Warren. Warren was a product of Sandhurst and the Royal Military Academy; he was a successful, but not a particularly lucky man. Warren set about organising the Metropolitan Police in the only way he knew, under military lines. 1887 was Queen Victoria's Jubilee year and he was going to ensure that there would be no repeat of the disorder of 1886. The police under Warren dealt with any signs of civil unrest very severely, using methods akin to an occupying army. This military mindset was likely to have had a direct effect on the attributes of its officers, with greater emphasis placed upon physical action rather than the more cerebral skills required for detection. As a direct result of Warren's leadership, the Met Police dealt brutally with the peaceful protestors who marched through Trafalgar Square on 13 November 1887. The police action was thought so unnecessary and brutal that the event was known thereafter as 'Bloody Sunday'. The name was to hold for nearly 100 years, only falling out of favour following the extreme public order measures used by the British Army to control demonstrators in Northern Ireland on 30 January 1972. The London based Star newspaper was fiercest in its criticism of treatment of the demonstrators, placing the blame squarely on shoulders of the Met's new commissioner, Sir Charles Warren, and his de facto boss, the Home Secretary, Sir Henry Matthews.

In addition to the docks, sources of work could be found in London's markets for meat, fish and fruit. Whitechapel had its own street markets, two of which are still in operation to this day, in Spitalfields and the Petticoat Lane (the area in and around Middlesex Street). Most of the jobs in the docks and markets went to men, and in the days before refrigeration most of the meat sold at the markets came from animals freshly butchered in numerous slaughterhouses, another male orientated environment. Much of the slaughterhouse work took place in the dark of the early hours of the morning, so the meat could be sold fresh on the day an animal was butchered. This meant that it was not an uncommon a sight to see bloodstained men walking the streets of the poorer districts of London as they made their way home after a nights work.

Jobs for unskilled women were few and far between, with most women in London under the age of 35 finding work in service in private households. Other women found work as seamstresses, laundresses, as cleaning ladies or by selling trinkets in markets and street corners.

The irregular incomes of many piecemeal workers did not allow them the luxury of secure rented accommodation. They were instead forced to pay for a bed on a nightly basis in what were formally called common lodging houses, but otherwise known as dosshouses - doss being the slang word for sleep. In the 1880s there were 240 pence in every pound. For 4d (four pence) a night a bed could be found in a dosshouse, sleeping ten or more people to a bedroom, in wooden beds resembling coffins. This accommodation was dirty, crowded, noisy and unsafe. However, as bad as it was, it was still more preferable to sleeping rough or enrolling at the dreaded workhouse.

Most of the fallen women of Whitechapel were women in their late 30s and early 40s. Most had in their early years, been married, had children and enjoyed relatively stable family lives. However, either by accident (death or unemployment of a spouse) or misadventure (taking to drink), these women had found their way to Whitechapel. Without regular means of employment, many of Whitechapel's women took to prostitution in order to get enough money for a few pints of ale, a shot of rum, a little food and bed for the night. Many of London's poor would drink themselves senseless as a means of escaping the harsh realities of their daily lives and public houses were numerous. As an example, Dorset Street (a road central to the story of the Whitechapel murders) was about 100 metres in length and contained three pubs amongst its numerous dosshouses.

Life in Whitechapel was extremely hard. Violence and premature death were regular occurrences, with the slitting of throats being a common method of murder. Law and order were maintained on London's streets by lone police officers patrolling their beats. However, certain streets in Whitechapel were considered almost to be no go areas, with the police patrolling roads like Dorset Street, Flower & Dean Street, Thrawl Street and Bell Lane in pairs. These streets formed much of what was to be called the 'Wicked Quarter Mile', an area where the poor were left to fend for themselves by any means available to them.

Thus in 1888, London's Whitechapel made the ideal killing ground for Jack the Ripper. Its smog filled poorly lit streets, with its many desperate, drunk, vulnerable women, made the perfect haunt for a serial killer. As if to set the scene for the series of gruesome murders to come, a play named Dr Jekyll and Mr Hyde opened at the Lyceum

Theatre. A monster had been created in London's theatreland, paralleling the emergence of a real life monster who was about to start roaming the streets of London's East End. It was going to be the fate of some of the fallen women of Whitechapel to encounter him.

CHAPTER THREE

Serial Killers - Childhood

There is no doubting that Jack the Ripper was a serial killer. Therefore, in order to help identify him (and it is very much more likely to be a him than a her) it makes sense to use the techniques of modern criminal psychology that were not available to police forces in 1888.

Valuable studies have been made by psychologists into the minds of serial killers through interviews conducted with some of the convicted killers. This work has led to scientific techniques used in psychological and geographical profiling. Psychological profiling has given insights into the minds and motivations of these killers. Studies have been made into their upbringing and family backgrounds showing patterns of behaviour that might act as triggers for their actions in later life. Alongside this, geographical profiling has provided insights into locations that these killers live, work and kill in.

It is believed that adults with psychopathic personalities are more likely to have come from poor families, with dominant mothers and absent fathers. However, medical studies are ongoing to try and find out whether severe personality disorders might be innate, arising from genetic defects rather than from a person's live experiences. A psychological test has been devised, the 'Startle Reflex Test', where a person's response to sudden, startling stimuli, such as sudden noise or sharp movement, can indicate their predisposition to psychopathic behaviour. In his book 'The Psychopath Test' Ron Johnson informs how he learnt from a researcher in the field of criminal psychology, Robert D. Hare, that when a psychopath sees a grotesque image like a crime scene photograph, he isn't horrified by it, but is instead is absorbed by it, being interested in how the gruesome injuries have been inflicted. The implication of this is that experiences that you or I might find shocking, would to a psychopath be considered only interesting or absorbing. The psychopath will study such images and instead of recoiling in horror, will instead analyse how cuts were made, or how damage might have been inflicted on a body by for example, the entry and exit of a bullet.

Another precursor of the personality of the adult psychopath is known as the 'MacDonald Triad'. The triad states that three behaviours: enuresis (bedwetting), cruelty to animals and pyromania; if occurring together during childhood will greatly increase the probability of episodic aggressive behaviour occurring in adult life. The belief being that whilst still a child, a person who eventually becomes an adult psychopathic murderer, will have started to fantasise about the acts he will go on to commit in later life. It is also believed that access to pornographic material can tip those of a psychopathic disposition over the edge into becoming sadistic serial murderers.

The above description of upbringing and behaviours are wide ranging, but provide us with a lens through which we can view Sir Henry Wellcome's background and life experiences.

CHAPTER FOUR

Early Life of Henry Wellcome

Henry Soloman Wellcome was born on 21 August 1853 in a log cabin amongst the forests of Almond in northern Wisconsin, USA. He was the second of two sons born to Solomon and Mary Wellcome, a highly religious couple. Solomon's father was an Adventist Church Minister and Solomon junior would one day follow in his footsteps. Most families in Almond set themselves up on small farming plots. Agricultural work would have been hard for a fit healthy man, but Solomon was a man of poor health and during the family's early years he struggled to make a living as a farmer.

In the 1850s, America was still a largely undiscovered country, with many families moving into the Wild West, settling on land previously occupied by the Native American Indians. On the whole, the American frontiers people lived in peace with the Indian tribes, with the Indians being happy to share some of their culture with the white settlers. However, there were also periods of friction between the different communities, usually resulting from the Indians losing access to their old hunting grounds or sacred religious sites. None of this was of importance to Solomon Wellcome, his family and the other inhabitants of Almond. They were far from the frontier, with their primary focus on reaping a good harvest and storing enough food to get through the harsh winters.

It was whilst he was still a young boy that Henry Wellcome experienced two events that were to mould his life and personality thereafter. The first of these events occurred when he was just four years old. The young Henry found an oddly chipped stone and taking a fancy to it, took it home to show his father what he had found. Solomon Wellcome informed his young son that the object was in fact an ancient tool and went on to tell the boy about its history and purpose. This included how it had been shaped by human hands thousands of years before and might have been used for crafting weapons or for slicing meat. The object was likely to have meant more to those ancient peoples than the invention of the electric telegraph meant to modern Americans of the day. This story fired up the young Henry's imagination and he never forgot it. From that point onward, Henry Wellcome started to become a collector of historical artefacts, and his collection would go on to include over one million items during his lifetime. He obtained only a few items in his childhood, but in adulthood, he would go on to spend huge sums of money, amassing so many objects that he would never see all of them with his own eyes. Many of the items were purchased on his behalf through overseas agents and were to remain sealed forever in the packing cases that they arrived in.

Wellcome's finding and keeping the ancient stone tool is significant to my story as it indicates that in his earlier years, Sir Henry Wellcome did not collect things for the sake of collecting. No, the items he collected back then had a meaning to him. I propose that just like a serial killer's trophies, the items that Wellcome saw and touched, allowed him in his mind's eye to visualise their use. So that when for example, he picked-up a surgical implement such as a scalpel, he could imagine himself cutting into someone's flesh with it, in much the same manner as the surgeon that owned it before him.

One of Henry Wellcome's uncles, Jacob, possessed a happy combination of talent, energy and entrepreneurial spirit. Jacob took a gamble in moving west to a town named Garden City, in the newly created state of Minnesota. Life was good to Jacob and in a short time he combined the setting-up of a drug and general store alongside his work as a successful frontier surgeon. It was this knowledge and the failure of his own potato crop that led in 1861 to Solomon Wellcome joining his brother, moving his family 300 miles further to the west, to Garden City.

The area in and around Garden City had previously belonged to various Indian tribes, including the Crow and the Winnebago. The Crow were aggressive in nature and tended to keep away from the white settlers, whereas the Winnebago were friendlier and willing to interact with the town's people. The young Henry and his older brother, George Theodore, born on 31 July 1851, had contact with members of the Winnebago tribe, who taught them how to ride horses, hunt and canoe. Life in Garden City was as hard as it was in Almond, but was also more varied and offered the young boys more scope for adventure. As for the ailing Solomon Wellcome, it brought him closer to his brother who would help him as best he could through the hard times that lay ahead.

In 1862 the second of the two major events that forged the pillars of the young Henry's personality occurred. A band of disaffected Sioux Indians from the woodlands around Garden City attacked the settlement, killing more than 1,000 settlers. The Indians murdered all in their path (men, women and children), being particularly cruel to the women. The young Henry, only just nine years old, helped a team of children cast bullets for the guns of Garden City's defenders. In addition to participating in a life and death battle for survival, he also assisted his uncle Jacob in administering emergency surgery to settlers wounded in the battles fought against the marauding Indians. Witnessing bodies shot with arrows, stabbed with hunting knives and smashed with axes, would have been a highly traumatic experience for an adult, so it can be assumed that it would have had a lasting effect on a young boy. This was confirmed years later by one of Sir Henry's biographers, Robert Rhodes James, who in his book 'Henry Wellcome' made reference to the adult Henry Wellcome looking back at these terrifying and horrific events and remembering them supposedly as the most interesting experience of his life. We are not able to psychoanalyse the long dead Sir Henry Wellcome, but I believe that psychologists and Ripperologists will find such comments of interest. Such an event and such a recollection, even if taken out of context, must provide us with some insight into how his mind worked and how he viewed the world in which he lived.

Solomon's ill health resulted in his giving-up farming, but fortunately he was able to work in his brother's drug store. He and Jacob were on good terms and in time Jacob allowed Solomon to become a part owner of the store. However, Solomon was never particularly successful and his family was likely to have been one of the poorest in Garden City. Over time Soloman turned to a religious vocation and became a poorly paid minister in an Adventist Church, this work resulting in his being frequently away from home, whilst he conducted religious meetings in distant parts of the State.

When Henry was aged thirteen years old he left school and started working in his Uncle Jacob's store. It was there amongst the mortars and pestles that Henry's interest in medicine and medical research started to flourish. In addition to compounding medicine from his uncle's prescriptions, he also accompanied Jacob on his rounds, watching as he splinted fractures or dressed wounds.

Around this time, Henry came into contact with the owner of a small pharmacy, H. J. Barton, an English chemist, who was originally from Leeds. Mr Barton gave Henry a copy of a book called 'Attfield's Chemistry' and he used this to create his own chemicals. He even conducted explosive experiments using ammonium nitrate, which according to Wellcome's biographer, Rhodes James, may have bordered very much on the dangerous side. Rhodes James went on to write that Wellcome used to indulge in less than popular practical jokes that angered his Adventist Minister father. For all this, Henry showed promise as an inventor and entrepreneur. Aged just 16, Henry was making and selling his own version of invisible ink, which he named 'Magic Ink'.

Although life in the backwater of Garden City was more varied than in Almond, it was too limiting for a young man of ambition and the young Henry went on to work and study in Rochester, Chicago and Philadelphia. It must be said that Wellcome sent home a significant proportion of his income to his family back in Garden City, but such selfless behaviour came at a cost. Another of Wellcome's biographers, Helen Turner, in her 'The Man, His Collection and His Legacy' writes about how poor Wellcome was, whilst trying to square the circle of having little income, sending money back home to his family and keeping enough money for himself to live on. However, the most important reference from her book comes from one of Wellcome's letters in which he wrote describing his situation. He informed, that being so poor meant that he had to wear what he called 'rubbers' over his boots in order to try and keep them together. Henry's poverty is not of interest to my theory, but covering his shoes and boots in thin skins of rubber is. In 1888, Jack the Ripper was thought to be able to walk noiselessly through the cobbled streets of Whitechapel, leading some to think that he might have lined the soles of his shoes with rubber. Back in 1874, a young Henry Wellcome would have been moving noiselessly through the streets of Philadelphia, not by design but as a result of relative poverty.

I believe it significant that even at the mature age of seventeen, Wellcome would still involve himself in some - not so harmless - pranks. Rhodes James made reference to a letter Henry received from his father, dated 31 April 1871, in which he was told off for lacing one of his letters with chilli peppers and so nearly putting out the reader's eyes. His father's letter also made reference to Henry being told to leave off his little tricks and jokes. So at the age of 17, when supposedly a diligent scholar and hardworking young man who sent all his spare money back home to his family, Henry Wellcome appears happy to have played his own funny little games on the folks back home. The information available about Wellcome's childhood was sparse. However, the information that is available appears to depict the young Henry Wellcome as a practical joker with a potentially vicious side to his personality.

It must also be noted that religion played a major part in Wellcome's upbringing. The communities that he grew up in were highly religious, as was his own family, with his father, grandfather and brother George all becoming ministers in the Adventist Church. Henry Wellcome himself was not a highly religious man, but he was unlikely to have been unaffected by being brought up in such puritanical surroundings.

All in all, the young Henry was a great success. In 1876, when aged 23, he had completed his studies and found employment in a firm named McKesson and Robbins, one of the foremost wholesale druggists in New York. He travelled extensively in his role for the company; travelling not only within the newly created United States, but also to South and Central America. He and his company's interest lay in chemical called quinine, which could be extracted from the bark of cinchona trees. Wellcome's passion for collecting all things medical had already begun. Following one of his treks he is said to have returned to New York with a large number of specimens and a collection of native surgical instruments. The young Henry has been described as being five feet eight inches in height, with blue eyes, ginger hair and a ginger moustache. He was also said to possess remarkable charm and had an aptitude for making valuable social and business contacts. I think that it is worth adding that he also had a passion for collecting surgical knives and may have spent time imagining how they were used before coming into his possession.

I was unable to discover anything of note about Henry's relationship with his mother. There was no mention of her being described as a domineering woman, but the same cannot be said for his grandmother, Mary Cummings Wellcome, who was thought to be a very domineering woman. By all accounts, when Mary Wellcome died she was not missed by anyone that she left behind.

My only comment on Henry's relationship with his mother is that there appears to have been some hidden problem with it. Henry rarely took time to visit her, even in later years when he was informed that she was seriously ill with cancer. He also did not travel to America for her funeral, yet on hearing the news of his brother George's death, he is said to have requested that the funeral be delayed in order to give him sufficient time in which to travel back to his native America from England so that he could attend the ceremony.

Although the above is a far from comprehensive description of the young Henry's early life, there is enough information to see how his sanity might have been damaged in his middle years. Wellcome had, a weak and mainly absent father, a passion for creating explosions and enjoyed hunting animals. We do not know if he suffered from enuresis, but his childhood was unusual in that at just nine years old, he most likely witnessed death and the gruesome injuries inflicted on the settlers of Garden City by rampaging Sioux Indians in 1862. His academic and business successes are definitely at odds with the profile of a sadistic serial killer. That said it is already apparent that he had a passion for performing what he felt to be tricks and jokes, enjoying making explosive and destructive chemical compounds and allegedly finding it funny that someone might put a chilli pepper covered finger in their eyes after reading one of his letters. His early interest in collecting surgical instruments might have seemed less unusual in the late nineteenth century than it does now in the twentyfirst century, however, I feel that it is this activity above all others that provides the key to understanding Wellcome's mindset.

I find it odd that anyone, after witnessing something as traumatic as death and surgery as a child, would go on to describe the experience as the most interesting of their early life. But then who knows how any of us would have been affected by the sight of semi-naked mutilated bodies of women, men and children when aged only nine years old?

I appreciate that it is a very large leap to take, but I propose that Henry Wellcome had a very vivid imagination and may have taken pleasure from visualizing the use the surgical knifes and other medical equipment that he purchased for his collection. Sadly, we will never know whether he really had any such thoughts, but what cannot be disputed is that he had a very keen interest in surgery, culminating in his being made an Honorary Fellow of the Royal College of Surgeons in March 1932.

CHAPTER FIVE

Sadistic Serial Killers – Into Dreamland

There are two types of serial killers, the organised and the disorganised. The organised killer will have a relatively stable personality, allowing him to hold down a regular job and come across as a personable person. When he kills he will have already pre-planned the when, where and how of the murder, but might well leave selection of the victim to a chance encounter. The disorganised killer's life will be a mess; he will have had trouble holding down a regular job and will be awkward in social interactions. When he kills, he will have a good idea of the where and how, but is likely to act on impulse and so not have too much control over date, time or the choice of victim to be killed. Our killer 'Jack the Ripper' is most likely in the first category, that of an organised killer. He might well have a target in mind and most likely have selected the when, where and how, in advance of committing an act of murder.

Joel Norris, in his book 'Serial Killers, The Growing Menace' has listed the following seven stages in the life of the Serial Killer: Aura, Trolling, Wooing, Capture, Murder, Totem and Depression. I've summarised the stages below:

Aura: This is a transition from reality into madness. A potential serial murderer will most likely have experienced murderous fantasies from childhood, but will not act on them until crossing a mental boundary, that facilitates the final descent that allows him to commit physical acts of murder.

Trolling: In this second stage the deranged individual is now fantasising about committing murder and will be actively planning where and how to commit the act. His fantasies will involve a certain 'type' of victim and he will likely visit the area where he is able to capture and possibly kill this 'type' of individual.

Wooing: The killer is now actively prowling his chosen zone of capture for a victim. It is important for the killer to be able to win the confidence of potential victims in order to manoeuvre them into his trap. He will use false charm to get them to lower their defences and trust him. Norris informs that this is a very important stage for an organised serial killer. It is almost as if the killer will only kill people who allow him to gain their trust. Tales of the fictional vampire are not too dissimilar in this, as the vampire of old needs to be invited into the home of their chosen victim before he or she is able to attack them.

Capture: This is a killer's favourite moment. It is at this stage he feels at his most powerful. Norris informs that at this stage the killer reveals his true purpose. To ensure capture he will then incapacitate his victim by physical or chemical means. He has control and will gain pleasure from his victim's physical and mental distress.

Murder: The modus operandi (MO) of the killer revolves around the ritual enactment of the killer's childhood fantasies. The method of murder might evolve over time to become more efficient, but the killer's dreams are the driving force for the physical act.

Totem: In this stage the act of murder is over. The killer has lost power over his victim, who no longer has the capacity to be afraid of him. His sense of excitement drops, and the killer returns from his fantasy back into the real world. Norris informs that the killer wants to relive the moment and may take a 'trophy' from the victim (an item of clothing, a body part, jewellery or a photograph) to re-enact the act of murder over and over again in his mind. Then, over time his sense of power will diminish and he will seek a new experience to satisfy his dysfunctional needs.

Depression: The life of the killer feels empty without the power obtained from the act of ritual murder. He will fall into a depression and will try to alleviate this by use of a trophy in the Totem phase. Eventually he will take action to break out of this phase, and revert to the trolling state, and so resume the spiral of death.

Norris says that the cycle of death, once started will continue until the killer is physically unable to catch his prey. It is very unlikely that he will be able to stop himself from killing. One can make the assumption that any serial killer capable of freeing himself from this spiral of death; will most likely spend the rest of his life in some form of depressed state.

Other experts in the field of severe personality disorder, John E Douglas et al, inform in the 'Crime Classification Manual: A standard system for investigating and classifying violent crime' that following the transfer to the aura stage, there can be what they term 'Precipitating Stressors', stressful situations that can push a potential killer through the mental barrier that has previously stopped him from committing murder. High on the list of such stressors, is the loss of financial security and status that would result from becoming unemployed. Sir Henry Wellcome's biographer, Rhodes James, was of the opinion that many of the greatest stresses in Wellcome's life emanated from his legal battles with Silas Burroughs, over the ownership their world beating company, Burroughs Wellcome and Co. The greatest of their ongoing legal battles happened to take place between the years of 1887 and 1889.

My thesis is that in the year 1888, having spent many months facing a huge threat to his status and financial security, something snapped in Henry Wellcome and he experienced what Norris terms the aura, which resulted in a mental collapse which took him into the realm of the sadistic serial murderer.

CHAPTER SIX

Burroughs Wellcome & Company

In 1878, when aged 25, Henry Wellcome was a rising star at the pharmaceutical company, McKesson and Robbins. A few years earlier he had made the acquaintance of another of the American Pharmaceutical Industry's rising stars, Silas Manville Burroughs. Silas Burroughs was seven years older than Wellcome, rich, educated and a specialist in the new field of compressed medicines - tablet drugs. Up until this time chemists and hospitals administered most drugs in liquid form, mixing chemicals as and when required, with variable dosages of the key components, leading to little or no consistency in the preparation of prescriptions. That said, in the 1870s, most medicines were very still quite basic, with tonics being the order of the day. Medical prescriptions were as likely to contain such innocuous substances as cod liver oil or malt extract, as say a powerful high dependency drug like morphine. In June 1878 Burroughs opened his small business, 'S.M. Burroughs & Company' in Southampton Street, just off the Strand in London. He had a licence to sell compressed medicines on behalf of the American based company John Wyeth and Brother. Wyeth's produced tablets in the United States, exporting them into the UK, where Burroughs sold them on under licence through his company to the UK market. Burroughs had grand plans and felt that there were many unexploited markets for tablet medicines. He quickly found his first premises too small to cope with the demand of the rapidly expanding UK market, so he moved into two rooms in Great Russell Street. In addition to this he rented a basement at 1 Cock Lane and used it as a warehouse and packing department. He would keep the warehouse well into the 1880s; which was walking distance from London's Whitechapel.

For all of his early success, Burroughs encountered a problem. Although as an American he was savvy in sales and marketing and had correctly identified the UK as a place that he could create a market for the medicinal products and cosmetics, his grand plan was to sell his products worldwide, in the markets of Europe and the New World. However, to gain access to overseas markets required his going on a worldwide promotional tour, which would include countries as far away as Australia and New Zealand. He was never going to be able to do that and manage his fledgling London based business at the same time. What he needed was a man of quality and integrity to run the London business in his long absence from Britain.

Burroughs had met and was friendly with Henry Wellcome, and knew him to be a rising star in the American pharmaceutical market. As such, he hit upon the idea of enticing Henry Wellcome over to England to help him run his London office. Wellcome still had nothing in the way of personal wealth, but he was doing very well for himself at McKesson and Robbins, and so needed a lot of persuading to give up his blossoming career and move to England. After much courting, Burroughs finally managed to persuade the young Henry to travel to England to discuss the possibilities of the two men working together.

Wellcome did not arrive in England empty-handed, he brought with him a trump card to play in his negotiations with Burroughs. He had no capital of his own, but on resigning from McKesson & Robbins he had managed to persuade his former employers to grant him the sole rights to sell their products in Europe, Asia, Africa, the East Indies and Australia. If Burroughs had been hoping to hire an employee, Wellcome had his own grand plans and was not willing to transfer continents just to move from one company for another; no, what Wellcome wanted was a business partnership. Finally an agreement was reached between the two men and the wealthy Silas Manville Burroughs and the penniless Henry Solomon Wellcome set-up in partnership. As was standard business practice, each of the two partners was required to invest their own capital in the firm. Wellcome had no money of his own to invest but he did have the sole rights to sell McKesson & Robbins' products, so Burroughs lent Wellcome the money he needed for his share of the business, resulting in the formation of a very one-sided business partnership.

Thus in 1880 the legendary pharmaceutical firm 'Burroughs Wellcome & Company' was created, with Silas Burroughs as its rich, well-connected senior partner. The unequal partnership served Burroughs' immediate requirements, in that it allowed him to set off on his worldwide promotional tour, leaving Henry Wellcome to deal with the day-to-day problems of managing the London based company.

Wellcome was as lucky in his business life as he was talented. He had a few years work experience working for McK & R, but his main responsibility had been sales, not management. As luck would have it, he inherited two very capable members of staff, both of whom had joined Burroughs' original company in 1879. Robert Clay Sudlow joined as a clerk when aged 33, and was an exceptionally capable man with abilities far exceeding those required by his post. He was the type of individual any new business would be lucky to have and was able to take on new roles and responsibilities, as and when demanded by the fast expanding business. Wellcome soon recognised Sudlow's talent and quickly promoted him to the position of General Manager, a position he held until his retirement in 1905. The second man of note was William Henry Kirby. Kirby had been employed in a similar capacity to Sudlow. He was not quite as talented, but nevertheless proved to be a capable, reliable and loyal employee. Kirby was to remain in the firm until his untimely death, due to a tragic accident, in September 1895.

Under Wellcome's stewardship, the company went from strength to strength. Wellcome had an eye for marketing and advertising, and focused all his efforts on gaining the attention of the British Medical Association to the company. His strategy included refusing to advertise the company's products to the general public, his reasoning being that to do so would reduce the company's status in the eyes of the professionals of the BMA. Wellcome was meticulous in his planning and showed great attention to detail, leaving nothing to chance. Examples of his fastidiousness can be found in his preparations for exhibitions held by the international pharmaceutical community. These events were de facto trade fairs and in August 1880 Wellcome started as he meant to continue, personally designing the Burroughs Wellcome exhibition of medicinal products at the annual BMA meeting held in Cambridge. Wellcome's exhibit caused a sensation, nothing like it had been seen before and it left a lasting impression in the minds of the BMA and healthcare community at large, with special reference made to it in the British Medical Journal. Later in the year, another of his displays won a Diploma of Honour at the Antwerp International Exhibition.

Burroughs on the other hand, was very much an ideas man. A typical example of this was in the marketing of a product named Hazeline - a liquid extracted from Witch Hazel bark. In 1880, the company was marketing the product as 'Burroughs' Hazeline' to women as a skin cream. Borroughs wrote to Wellcome from New Zealand in 1882 and from Australia in 1883 with his ideas for selling the product in new ways. His thinking was that Hazeline might also be sold as a hair-restorer or a treatment for piles. Having thought-up other uses for the product, he left Wellcome to implement and make money out of them.

Outside of work, Wellcome quickly settled into London life. He had sufficient money left over from Burroughs' loan to rent accommodation in Bury Street, close to well-heeled St James Square. His funds allowed him to hire staff to assist with cooking, cleaning and the entertainment of guests. He took to sailing in the Norfolk Broads and the English Channel and particularly enjoyed canoeing on the river Thames. He had enjoyed canoeing since childhood and would one day own a small fleet of purpose built American Indian style canoes. He was also said to enjoy spending his time in the company of actors and actresses, much more so the ladies than the gentleman. In 1881 he moved to rented accommodation on the Marylebone Road, close to Madame Tussaud's waxworks. Included in the decoration of his new home was a collection of what Wellcome termed his 'curiosities' or 'curios' and included his American Indian relics and old medical instruments. Wellcome had brought a few artefacts over from America and appears to have lost no time in purchasing additional macabre pieces for his collection. It is my belief that this shows that Wellcome was already very passionate about collecting old, used medical instruments and artefacts relating to the American Indians. There is of course nothing wrong with such interests. However, I find it strange that the young Henry would want to collect items that would clearly have reminded him of the death and destruction wrought on the inhabitants of Garden City by the Sioux Indians.

In the dog-eat-dog world of business, Boroughs Wellcome & Co's early advantage over their competitors lay in their having new products with unique names. Both Burroughs and Wellcome had learnt all about the power of brand loyalty back in America and were very careful to create and protect branded products. In 1878 Burroughs had secured trademark protection for the name 'tablet', which he applied to Wyeth's compressed medicines that he had licence to sell in Britain and Europe. However, competition from other firms was fierce, especially after the introduction of the Patents, Designs and Trademarks Act of 1883. This led in 1884 to Wellcome inventing the word 'Tabloid' as the name relating specifically to Burroughs Wellcome & Company's compressed medicines. The company finally had a trade name that their competitors could not use. If they tried to, Burroughs Wellcome & Co lost no time in taking them to court.

Things were going well for the new business but it was all done at the expense of Wellcome's health. Whilst Burroughs travelled the world, thinking-up new ideas for products, Wellcome was left at home with the difficult task of trying to make money from them. Rhodes James recorded that Wellcome wrote to a friend in October 1882 complaining that he and his colleagues were working like dogs but achieving far lower results than he would have expected in America. However, it must be noted that when in America, Wellcome was an employee, whereas, despite the hardships he endured in England, he had the added incentive of knowing that as a partner in a business, his efforts might potentially make him massive financial gains. However, Wellcome, just like his father before him, was susceptible to bouts of ill health and he was not slow in letting people know when he was feeling unwell.

In spite of the difficulties, the firm continued to expand and in 1884, the firm set-up headquarters in what Burroughs termed the 'Boss' drug premises in London's Snow Hill. Wellcome controlled all arrangements of the internal design of the building, which included the bold decision to install Edison's new invention of electric light. A new purpose built factory was also established in Bell Lane, Wandsworth, which in 1883, was considered to be a country location on the outskirts of London, south of the River Thames.

In the midst of what appears to be the frenetic activity

of building-up a new business, Wellcome also managed to maintain as equally frenetic social life. However, there are hints that he experienced difficulty in trying to burn the candle at both ends.

Wellcome was thought to be a confirmed bachelor and gave no hint of ever getting married until he was well into his forties. In 1882 he was to strike-up a lifelong friendship with a married woman, Mrs May French Sheldon, who was married to a successful businessman named, Eli. The Sheldons were American, which would have given them added appeal to Wellcome. Mrs Sheldon was famous for her travel writing and had already been on four world tours by the time Wellcome made her acquaintance. Wellcome appears to have been attracted to Mrs Sheldon and rumours circulated of their having an affair. The Sheldons and others in Wellcome's social circle appear to have kept very late hours. Rhodes James has written that Burroughs was to accuse Wellcome of consistently arriving late into the office upon his return from America in 1887, with Wellcome supposedly not arriving into work before 11.00am due to his attendance at late night gatherings with his friends. Rhodes James provided details of a conversation that Burroughs had in a chance encounter with Wellcome's landlady at a ball in 1884. Wellcome appears to have been struggling with ill health and Burroughs, probably concerned about his business partner's welfare, must have asked the lady if she knew of any possible cause for Wellcome's ill health. She is supposed to have opined that, 'there was nothing wrong with him that could not be cured by his going to bed at a reasonable hour and getting up in good time for work, instead of staying-up most of the night with literary people and then lying in bed all day'. Burroughs is unlikely to have been best pleased to hear such a comment made about his ailing business partner's personal life.

The profiles of Jack the Ripper have suggested that he

most likely held down a regular Monday to Friday job. Now, if the Ripper was an organised serial killer, and it is thought that he was, then he is likely to have planned his attacks, spending a number of late nights out in Whitechapel selecting the locations for his murders. Such activity is unlikely to have helped with his time keeping and so might have resulted in a number of late arrivals into work. Now, I am not suggesting that in 1884 Wellcome was already planning the murder of Whitechapel prostitutes, but it is possible that he was doing more than that just socialising with friends on his late nights out in London.

So in 1884, we have Wellcome burning the candle at both ends, beginning to become ill and arriving late into work. In spite of this, he managed to ensure that the company went from strength to strength. He would most likely have expected his business partner to be pleased with the progress made by the organisation, but Burroughs never appeared to be satisfied with the state of the company. Rhodes James hints that Burroughs business relationship with Wellcome was frosty, with his often shouting at Wellcome, using bad and offensive language.

It is highly likely that Burroughs reluctantly entered into partnership with Wellcome, as he had no other means of persuading him to run the company for him during his absence from the country. If that was the case, then it is quite likely that he planned to dissolve their partnership upon his return to England, when he was again able to direct operations in person. Burroughs' actions upon his return to England would appear to confirm this, with there being a number of examples of Burroughs' trying to wrest back control of the firm from Wellcome. In 1883 Burroughs tried to make a fellow American, John Van Schaack, a partner of the firm, which would have resulted in his reducing Wellcome's stake in the company. In 1884 he proposed turning the firm into a limited liability company with the object that he and his associates would have a controlling interest. In both instances, Wellcome rejected the proposed changes to the company's management structure and operational status. However, it must have been becoming patently obvious to him that all was not well with his business relationship with Burroughs. After spending years of his life working like a dog, trying to establish the company's reputation and to make a decent return on 'their' investment, Wellcome was not going to be easily pushed aside. He was becoming an astute businessman and stuck carefully to the letter of the law when fending off Burroughs' proposed changes to their business affairs.

Burroughs' attempts to wrest the company from Wellcome coincided with an event that was to have lasting significance in the men's future working relationship. In February 1883 Borroughs wrote to Wellcome informing him that he intended to get engaged to a lady named Olive Chase. Wellcome's reaction to the news was a little odd and certainly would not have been expected by his senior business partner. Wellcome wrote back saying that he felt the engagement to Burroughs' 'Olive Branch' would be a mistake. It is almost as if Wellcome had felt betrayed by the actions of his business partner. As can be expected, Burroughs took no notice of Wellcome and got married in February 1884, bringing his bride to England in March 1884. The result of Wellcome's reaction to his business partner's engagement was to place an unnecessary additional burden upon him. Up until 1884 working with Burroughs had been difficult but manageable. From that point onwards, Wellcome not only had to contend with a difficult senior partner, but also his irate wife. We do not know if Burroughs ever showed his future wife Wellcome's letter, but it is likely that he did so. All that is known is that Mrs Burroughs made it very clear to Wellcome that she did not like him.

By 1885 Wellcome had put his all into establishing

Burroughs Wellcome & Company as a market leader in the manufacture and retail of compressed medicines and tonics. His efforts had not been in vain. Thanks mainly to him, the firm was selling patent protected compressed medicines, had fast expanding sales, had set-up a new London based factory in Wandsworth and had established a new 'Boss' HQ in Central London. Wellcome had achieved much of this whilst working at arm's length from a highly critical business partner, who following his engagement and marriage appeared intent on wresting control of the company from him. Wellcome for his part appears to have embraced London's social scene with gusto, resulting in his keeping odd hours, arriving late for work and staying out half the night, supposedly in the company of his literary friends.

I suggest that by 1885 Henry Wellcome was a man who may have spent many years fantasising about surgical objects and the performance of surgery procedures. He had spent years working under great stress and was likely further stressed by actions of his business partner. Such feelings of insecurity could only have been escalated by Burroughs' actions following his engagement and marriage to Olive Chase. None of this would have been helped by Wellcome's keeping late nights, further draining his physical and mental capabilities. Wellcome appears to have been struggling physically, but up until that point he had just about been able to cope. Now under the additional pressure caused by the potential loss of his life's work he may have snapped. It was at this point in his life when he might have teetered on the brink of what Joel Norris terms the 'Aura', the transition into insanity. If so, once across that mental line it would only be a matter of time before he would commit the physical act of murder.

CHAPTER SEVEN

1885 – Freemasonry and the Ripper

In 1885 Wellcome's general manager, Robert Sudlow, introduced him to Freemasonry. He was to become a very active Mason and rose rapidly through the organisation's ranks. His other loyal employee, William Kirby, was also an enthusiastic Mason. Both Sudlow and Kirby had by this time become personal friends of Wellcome's and it was through them and Freemasonry that he was introduced to influential elements of British society. Unfortunately, I have not found any documentation shedding light on how quickly Wellcome rose through the ranks of the Masons, so I do not know what level he reached within this shadowy organisation. However, it is likely that by 1888, within three years of becoming a member of an English Masonic Lodge, that Henry Wellcome would have passed through Freemasonry's Royal Arch, meaning that he had joined its senior ranks.

It is my theory that Henry Wellcome may have been fantasising about performing surgery on women since the age of nine, when he had assisted his uncle Jacob in the tending of the wounded of Garden City following the savage attacks launched by the Sioux Indians. Then, at the age of 32, Wellcome is introduced to an organisation whose initiation ceremonies are rumoured to include the acting out of the scenes of ritual murder. Supposedly, the ceremonies demonstrated how members' who betray the organisation should be punished and are said to include evisceration of the betrayer's body cavity and the throwing the victim's entrails over the shoulder of their prostrate bodies. The vast majority of Masons are likely to have found such ceremonies a little odd, and simply part of a means to an end. To a man like Henry Wellcome, a man whose early life was likely scarred by the evisceration of human bodies, participation in such ceremonies may have left him feeling closer to fulfilling a special destiny.

Freemasonry has the potential to play many roles in the Whitechapel murders. What is definitely known and cannot be disputed is that the two most senior members of the Metropolitan Police, the Commissioner, Sir Charles Warren, and his deputy, Dr Robert Anderson, were both very senior Freemasons. Knowledge of this has led many to question the motives behind the decisions taken by these two men during the investigation into the Whitechapel murders. It has been proposed that they even knew the identity of the murderer and did not divulge it because he was a fellow Freemason, with one theory going so far as to propose that Dr Anderson was actually involved in the murders.

The positions held by people within the Masonic Hierarchy are called Degrees. Most Masons are aware of and aspire to achieving the bottom three degrees of Freemasonry, which in increasing seniority, are the Entered Apprentice, Fellowcraft Mason, and Master Mason. However, much less well known is that there are 33 degrees in the total hierarchy, there being another thirty degrees above the rank of Master Mason. With these higher ranks only being open to Freemasons attending the most influential lodges. The first step (fourth degree) on the long climb to the rank of 'Most Puissant Sovereign Commander' is the rank of Royal Arch Mason, a level likely open to someone like Wellcome who would have attended one of the influential London based lodges.

As I have already alluded to, initiation ceremonies in Masonry's junior ranks are said to include the miming of the act of murder, with the ripping open the abdomen and throwing the entrails over the victim's shoulder. So it well within the bounds of possibility that one rogue member, out of many thousands, might one day become mad and embark on a killing spree, murdering his victims in the fashion similar to the rituals enacted in its initiation ceremonies.

Ripperologist, Stephen Knight was very aware of the workings of the Brotherhood. He investigated the practices of the organisation in order to give credence to his claim that a few rogue Freemasons were responsible the Whitechapel murders. His thesis was that the killing of five Whitechapel prostitutes was part of a scheme to protect the British Royal Family from scandal. Knight states in his book 'Jack the Ripper - The Final Solution', that at the initiation ceremony of a fourth degree Royal Arch Mason, the initiate 'must swear total loyalty to all other Masons of equal standing, murder and treason included'. So to Knight's understanding, once a Mason has passed through the Royal Arch, he ceases to be a normal citizen of a nation state, in that his primary loyalty is to the Brotherhood. In Knight's version of events, Dr Robert Anderson, the Deputy Commissioner, actually takes part in the plot to capture and murder of Whitechapel prostitutes. More about his theory can be found in the appendix to this book.

We already know that by 1885 Wellcome had a keen interest in surgery and was a collector of 'medical' artefacts. He was now introduced into a world that might further feed his fantasies, as the initiation ceremonies of Freemasonry are believed to include the miming of gruesome murders. 1885 was also the year that Burroughs chose to up the ante and formally tried to dissolve his partnership with Wellcome and claim back control of 'his' company. On 7 January Wellcome received a letter from Burroughs' solicitors, stating that Burroughs was dissatisfied with the company accounts and also requested that Wellcome immediately add more capital to the firm as specified by the company's Deed of Partnership. This letter appears to have been written, firstly to imply impropriety and incompetence on Wellcome's part; secondly to remind Wellcome that he was not an equal partner in the business; and thirdly to place Wellcome under some financial stress. One thing that is certain, is that Wellcome would have felt financial stress, as from out of the blue he was suddenly expected to stump-up a not inconsiderable some of money required to top-up his capital contribution to the business.

The end result of Burroughs' action was that a new Deed of Partnership was drawn-up, with additional capital inputs required by both partners. However, this deed included a clause that no longer allowed Wellcome the option of becoming an equal partner by the purchase of additional shares. The deed also allowed for the partnership to be terminated by either party at the end of five years. So in 1885, Burroughs had sown the seed for the possible dissolution of the partnership in the year 1890.

1885 is also the year that Rhodes James states that Wellcome developed a physical illness named ulcerative colitis, an illness that was to go undiagnosed for thirteen years. In September of that year Wellcome's illness is said to have reached crisis point and was not helped by an act of bravery that went on to undermine his physical capabilities.

Wellcome was an expert canoeist and by this time owned a number of authentic American Indian canoes, which he, business contacts and friends would use on the River Thames. It was on one such trip along the river, with an American authoress, a Miss Wakeman, that disaster struck. Miss Wakeman's canoe sank when the floodgates of a lock were opened, the current sucking her under the surface. By all accounts, she would most likely have drowned if she had not been saved by Wellcome. Wellcome's act of heroism did not go unnoticed and the story was reported in newspapers and he even went on to receive the Royal Humane Society's Bronze Medal for bravery for his selfless act. However, despite all the attention received for this great deed, all was not well with Wellcome. Rhodes James' biography includes a letter written by Wellcome in which he alluded to the massive physical effort that he had used to save Miss Wakeman's life. Wellcome's health deteriorated rapidly after that incident and resulted in his two loyal colleagues, friends and fellow Freemasons, Sudlow and Kirby, informing Burroughs that Wellcome was overdoing things. I believe that they did this, not only because Wellcome was most likely arriving late into work and looking physically ill, but also because of mental changes that they could see taking place within him. Wellcome's doctor was in agreement with their assessment and advised him to take a long break away from work. Burroughs agreed to this and Wellcome made arrangements for an open-ended break, in an effort to regain his health.

So in 1885 we have in Henry Wellcome, an angry and ill man. He was angry with Burroughs and probably even angrier with Burroughs' wife Olive, whom he likely saw as the instigator of the schemes to remove him from the two mens successful business. He was now suffering from an undiagnosed illness, which had the effect of draining his usual high reserves of energy. It is my belief that the perfect storm of events were now starting to take their toll on Wellcome. In addition to being angry, ill and insecure, he might also have been experiencing fantasies that included performing surgery and killing women using the methods of Masonic ritual. It is my contention that if Wellcome was ever to become the evil sadistic killer of women known as Jack the Ripper, he would in 1885 be close to what Joel Norris terms the aura – the final transition into madness. Burroughs had now applied enough external pressure through his efforts to wrest back his business, to push Wellcome over the edge. I propose that if Wellcome had not listened to his trusted friends and taken a break from his working duties, the Whitechapel murders might have started two years earlier, in the year 1886. However, Wellcome did take a break from work and went sailing around the Isle of Wight between May and July of 1886, before returning to his native America in August of that year.

In 1886, Wellcome returned to America but instead of heading straight to his family home, as might have been expected of an ill man, he spent his first few days booked into the same hotel as his good friend Mrs May Sheldon. This and his staying at the home of her mother and her sister later in the year, were to fuel rumours that he was having an affair with her, but nothing was ever proved. For a man supposedly too ill to work, Wellcome somehow summoned the energy to help Mrs Sheldon with a book she was writing, a translation of Flaubert's 'Salammbo', a book considered by many in the 1880s to be an obscene publication. The Sheldons bought an interest in a publishing company named 'Saxon & Company' as a means of getting May's book published, greatly assisted by Wellcome, who provided some of his own capital for the purchase. The book went on to be a huge a success, due in no small part to Wellcome's energetic promotion in England and America.

Whilst away from home, Wellcome literally had time to kill. In October and November 1886 he went to Maine, spending his time hunting and canoeing. Although not keen to return to London and the pressures of work, Wellcome seemed unable to relax for long, and on his return from his trip to the woods he seems to have caught the publishing bug as he decided to write a book of his own. Wellcome always had a fondness for the Native American Indians, and decided late in 1886 to support a campaign launched on their behalf by a lay missionary, Father William Duncan. Father Duncan had converted a large number of Tsimshian Indians to Christianity, but try as he might they would not follow all the rules of the religion. This did not go down well with members of the Church Missionary Society, an organisation that had been funding the tribe's accommodation. The society decided that as the Indians were not 'true' Christians, it could no longer support them and withdrew its funding of the tribe's accommodation and more importantly, reclaimed the land that the settlement had been living on. This forced Father Duncan to instigate a search for land suitable for the resettlement of the tribe and he sourced a suitable site on Annette Island, Alaska. Having no money of his own, he appealed to the Government of the United States to vote the land over to the Tsimshian Indians and his appeal gained much more weight after Wellcome joined his plan to seek US protection for the settlement. The two men travelled to Washington, where Duncan presented his petition to members of the Supreme Court and the Senate. Wellcome, ever the publicist, decided to publicise the plight of the Indians by writing a book 'The Story of Metlakahtla', publishing it through the publishing company he purchased with the Sheldons, Saxon & Company. Wellcome had never lost anything in his life and as might be expected, his and Father Duncan's campaign was a great success, with the American authorities passing new legislation that allowed Duncan and 800 Indians to move to the 'New Metlakahtla' settlement in 1887.

We do not know what Silas Burroughs' true intentions were with respect to the company he owned with Henry Wellcome, but it is possible that he intentionally gave Wellcome enough hypothetical rope with which to hang himself, with his agreement to his business partner's open ended leave of absence. Wellcome's filling his time 'struggling' through illness by: helping his 'good friend' Mrs May Sheldon buy shares in a publishing company so that she could publish a book; write and publish his own book; campaign in Washington on behalf of a group of American Indians; and spending most of the rest of his time hunting in the woods of Maine; would have provided pretty strong evidence of his being not being half as ill as he told everyone he was. But 1887 was the year that he made a formal legal challenge against Wellcome. In parallel to this, Burroughs also attempted to make a major decision behind Wellcome's back, with his trying to set-up a manufacturing plant in America. Burroughs actually went as far as travelling to America to source a suitable location for his and 'his partner's' new factory.

Wellcome was likely notified of Burroughs' intentions by Sudlow or Kirby and travelled to New York in the expectation of meeting Burroughs when the ship docked in the US. However, Wellcome guessed incorrectly, as Burroughs did not land in the US's business capital but instead travelled directly to Maine, a state he thought ideal for the production of products from malt extract. The upshot of this was that they missed each other. So on 2 May 1887 Wellcome wrote to Burroughs, informing him that he was keen to meet with him as he had hardly received any information from him about the business since leaving England in August 1886.

Wellcome went on to discover from Sudlow and Kirby that during his absence Burroughs had been skilfully undermining his position in the firm and his reputation in the medical profession. He now realised that his long absence from the company, coupled with his other non-work related activities had provided Burroughs with enough ammunition with which to mount a serious bid to dissolve their business partnership. Wellcome decided to return at once to England, boarding a ship bound for London, on 25 June 1887.

At the end of July 1887 Burroughs started his attack on Wellcome in earnest. He sent Wellcome a letter informing him that in response to his not fulfilling his business obligations, he had taken the decision to dissolve their association. Burroughs then instructed his solicitors to initiate formal proceedings to dissolve their Deed of Partnership. Wellcome was now under massive stress, for the first time he was unsure whether the letter of the law was on his side and must have felt that Burroughs' wealth and influence might be the deciding factor in the outcome of their legal battle. However, the process was slow and painful and would drag on until June 1889, with the heights of their battles taking place during the summer of 1888. During this time Wellcome was under relentless pressure, he was no doubt now a man of means but was finding it difficult to fund all the legal costs relating to the case. It appeared to him that Burroughs planned to simultaneously sully his reputation in British medical circles and drain his financial resources, leaving him with nothing for all of his endeavours.

In the midst of all this, it was business as usual. Wellcome had persuaded Burroughs to forgo the idea of a new factory in America, and they instead agreed to open a new larger factory in England, replacing the factory in Wandsworth, which was now too small to meet the increasing demand for their products. However, all this involved more work. In the summer of 1888 the company purchased land at Phoenix Mills, Dartford, to the East of London and Burroughs and Wellcome almost immediately set about making detailed plans for the new factory. 1888 was also the year that the company finally broke away from their obligations to American company John Wyeth & Brother. This meant that they could now manufacture and sell all their own products, greatly enhancing their profit margins, but at the risk that they now had no stakeholders to support them in times of trouble. The split with Wyeth's was acrimonious, but Wellcome had never much cared for the company, as the quality of their products had been low.

So we now have a timeline of events from the year 1885 up until 1888 that show how Henry Wellcome may have been on the edge of a mental collapse. I propose that in 1885 Wellcome was on the verge of a mental breakdown, but was able to recover from it because he took a very lengthy leave of absence from work. However, from the summer of 1887 onwards, Wellcome was to have no respite from the pressures that were inadvertently affecting his health. As such, he may have spent a number of years straddling the boundary that separates an angry, disturbed individual, from crossing the over into the realm of the sadistic serial killer. His long break from work would have helped him maintain some peace of mind for a few additional years, but would only have served to defer the inevitable outcome of his upbringing. Burroughs' prolonged legal assault from 1887 had the effect of grinding Wellcome down and in the spring of 1888 I propose that something finally snapped in his mind and he crossed over the boundary into insanity.

CHAPTER EIGHT

1888 – Tipping Point

Henry Wellcome was now under immense strain. His mind was likely filled with his fantasies relating to the performance of surgery. He was very angry with his business partner and especially his business partner's wife, whom he felt had driven a wedge between them. He had been relatively well-off, but was now watching his income being drained away by legal fees and would have felt anger at being poor compared to Burroughs and to cap it all, he was sick and did not know the cause of his illness. Rhodes James says that that 1888 was the year in which Wellcome's dispute with Burroughs reached its peak. We can only assume that he was becoming highly stressed about the outcome of their ongoing legal battle. If ever there was going to be a year in which Wellcome was to experience significant precipitating stressors that could lead to mass murder, 1888 was it.

I propose that in April 1888 Wellcome reached a tipping point. On the night of Easter Monday on 3 April a Whitechapel prostitute, Emma Smith, was attacked and fatally injured by a gang of three men. The newspapers reported that crime in some detail, including that Emma lived in George Street, Whitechapel. The stories included details of the fatal injury, including the ramming of the object into her vagina. Details of this particularly brutal murder would have appalled most normal people. However, one reader was not appalled, he had been fantasising about women and surgery; the story fed his fantasies and he knew what he must do. The Ripper was a meticulous planner. He would not simply go into a neighbourhood that he did not know and try and lure women to their deaths. No, he was much cleverer than that.

As for Emma Smith, her story is a harrowing one. After the assault, she managed to drag herself to her common lodging house. The cost of a bed for the night was 4d and the money had to be paid in advance. Payments were the responsibility of the lodging house deputies and they thought nothing of turning men, women and children out into the streets if they did not have their night's doss; sometimes for people to die from exposure. So what a penniless Emma Smith thought would be done for her is not known, but what is known is that even in the hard uncompromising world of the 1880s, she did find help. The lodging house deputy, a Mary Russell and two fellow lodgers helped Emma walk slowly to Whitechapel's London Hospital. In 1888, hospitals were places in which poor people often went to die, and so it was that Emma Smith died there of her gruesome injuries.

I believe that from April 1888, the Ripper started to stalk Whitechapel. It was far from unusual for city gents to frequent the area, as it was fashionable for the rich and well to do, to go on social outings to London's rookeries. Omnibus trips could be booked for those fearful of sharing the streets with the wretches that inhabited them. These daytrips to London's rookeries would have been viewed by London's well-to-do in the similar vein to a modern day family outing to a zoo.

A fascination with the East End had started in the 1860's when a journalist, James Greenwood, caused more than a stir with his serialised story of his spending a single night in a London workhouse. It appears that his tale of being crammed into a workhouse bedroom with muscular rough men, proved addictive reading for the gentleman readers of the Pall Mall Gazette. So much was made of the story that it was even made into the theatrical production. Visits to the rookeries were given the name 'slumming' and activities ranged from the harmless gawping by omnibus passengers, to well to do men spending drunken nights out gambling and having sex with prostitutes. The fact that all of London's rookeries and Whitechapel in particular, were dangerous places to visit, only seems to have added to their attraction. In modern times the fascination with the nation's poor is still with us and the term 'poverty porn' has been invented to describe the numerous television programmes depicting the lives of the underclass.

It is likely that from the month of April 1888, the Ripper would start spending the odd late night out surveying the streets of Whitechapel. He would have watched where and how the whores did their business and may have followed police officers as they paced their beats, noting their habits, patterns and shift changes. Time passed quickly, it would soon be time of the August bank holiday, when he would be ready for work.

Burroughs maintained relentless pressure on Wellcome, with his solicitors churning out legal letters, all of which required legal responses by Wellcome's own solicitors and would have eaten into a greater proportion of the junior partner's income. Burroughs was rich, so would not have felt the money draining from his coffers, not so Wellcome, he was well aware of the cost of solicitors' fees and legal letters. He wrote to one of his friends saying that he felt it was Burroughs' plan to bleed him dry and so weaken his resolve. On top of this were the personal attacks. In Church and Tansey's book 'Burroughs Wellcome & Co. - Knowledge, Trust, Profit and the Transformation of the British Pharmaceutical Industry 1880-1940', they provide a flavour of the battle between the two men. They state that Burroughs' attacks on Wellcome were not limited to work, where he accused Wellcome of deceit and neglecting correspondence in his business affairs. No, they also included attacks on his personal life, with allegations of womanising and association with 'gay women' - a euphemism for prostitutes. No proof of this activity was provided, but if true, had Wellcome spent late evenings slumming in Whitechapel's East End?

The murder of Emma Smith had occurred during the April bank holiday weekend and prompted the Ripper to strike over the August bank holiday weekend. Like any organised serial murderer, he would have walked the streets of Whitechapel by day and night, in order to gain familiarity with the layout of the streets and the activities of the prostitutes and the policemen. The police worked three, eight hour shifts: 10.00pm to 6.00am, 6.00am to 2.00pm and 2.00pm to 10.0pm; with double the number of officers on the beat during the night shift. Each officer would take about 15 minutes to cover his beat, walking at a steady pace of about 2.5 mile per hour. Officers were issued with hobnailed boots which made a loud distinctive sound on Whitechapel's cobbled streets. No doubt the sound of a burley policeman pounding his beat would have served to both reassure the public and deter criminals. However, this would make evasion a simple task for a killer like the Ripper, giving him plenty of time to slip into the shadows on hearing the sound of a Beat Officer's slow measured footsteps. The Ripper could not have failed to notice the fixed beats of the policemen and that most public houses' were licensed for business until 12.30am. Therefore, the last real chance for the women of the night to make some money would have been between 12.30am and 1.00am, as the last of the drunken men made their way home or found a bed for the night in one of the many common lodging houses. A few of the chandler's shops would still be open for business for anyone wanting groceries or general supplies and a few pubs (like the Ten Bells) were allowed special licence to remain open for the night workers. However, in the main, the streets would have been pretty much deserted from about 1.00am onwards.

The Ripper's lust for murder would have been high, but

it was the planning of his gruesome acts that would have fulfilled his fantasies. He is likely to have been walking a tightrope of control, as opportunities to savage one lone prostitute after another must have presented themselves to him many times over, during the nights that he spent planning his first murder. He would have noted that life in Whitechapel was grim; violence and aggression were commonplace, and domestic arguments were often public and spilled out onto the streets. He knew that he would have to strike with speed and force, so as not to give his victims the chance to scream. However, he would have witnessed with his own eyes and ears how scuffles between men and women went unheeded, so any last gasp cries for help would most likely be ignored by the residents of neighbourhoods who heard them; as they would have heard it all before. He knew that his prey would be desperate for money, as any woman out past 1.00am would be very aware that her chance of 'earning' the money she needed for a bed for the night was dwindling fast. Such woman would take chances and could be led off into nice secluded spots where no one would interrupt him during the completion his work.

CHAPTER NINE

Martha Tabram – A Fumble in the Dark

Martha Tabram (nee White) was 39 years old and was a Londoner, born off the London Road in Southwark. She stood about 5 feet 3 inches in height, had dark hair and a dark completion. Her parents separated in 1869 when she was 16, with her father dying later in the same year. Life was hard, but there was no sign of the horrors to come when on Christmas Day 1869 Martha married Henry Samuel Tabram. In February 1871 she gave birth to their first child, a boy they named Frederick John. In December 1872 they had their second child, another boy who they named Charles Henry. But all was not well in the marriage and in 1875 Henry left Martha due to her heavy drinking. For three years Henry provided Martha with an allowance of 12 shillings a week, after which time he reduced it to 2s 6d a week. In 1879 Henry learned that Martha was living with another man named William Turner and so ceased payments to her altogether. Henry rarely saw Martha after 1879, and the last time they met was in the Whitechapel Road in December 1887, and she was drunk.

Martha's relationship with William Turner was also troubled by drink. They often separated, Martha having a tendency to go out drinking at night and not return until late the following day. On 6 August 1888 William and Martha were going through another of their separations. They had previously been living together in Star Street, off the Commercial Road, but now William was living at the Victoria Working Men's Home and Martha was living in a common lodging house at 19 George Street. Martha's dosshouse just happened to be opposite the one frequented by the ill-fated Emma Smith.

Wellcome lived close to Regents Park, a salubrious part of old London town where a blood-stained man was likely to stand out like a sore thumb. At a distance of over three miles from Whitechapel, it was too far for him to risk using as a base. Travelling such a distance in the early hours of the morning holding the real risk of his being stopped, searched and questioned by the police. So he planned on using one of the surgeon's knives housed in his grisly collection of curios, that he kept in his Snow Hill 'Boss' HQ office, a building less than half the distance from his home to Whitechapel. He knew that he was likely to get some blood on his person, so he prepared a change of clothes at the firm's basement warehouse, around the corner in Cock Lane. He kept some of his curious in the warehouse, so nobody there was going to give another surgical knife a second glance. Once cleaned-up he would have the option of returning to his business premises in Snow Hill, where he could bed down in his office, or he could travel the extra mile and a half to his home address.

✧ ✧ ✧

Then the great day finally arrived, and what a perfect day for the Ripper it was, with the 6 August bank holiday Monday being cool and cloudy with a high probability of rain. The bad weather was not going to stop the masses from enjoying the day and it would give the Ripper an excuse to wear a long coat in the middle of summer. No man would look out of place in a light raincoat on that grey cool summer's night. It would be just to thing to keep the blood off of his clothes.

The Ripper collected a surgeon's knife from his collection, the long 10-inch blade was awkward but fitted snugly inside his coat pocket. He was now ready and set-off for his night's work. He arrived in Whitechapel as darkness fell. He had dressed down a little so as not to attract too much attention to himself, but the quality of his clothes still made him immediately recognisable to the fallen women of Whitechapel, as another toff out on a night's slumming. He had spent many a night wandering the streets but now he was nervous. Being a bank holiday there were a lot more people about than was usual but fortunately many were the worse for drink. His biggest problem was the possibility of being accosted by some street toughs as he wandered in and out of the side streets, but this was a price he was willing to pay. He had set his sights on one of the George Street whores and may have wandered through there to fuel his fantasies, but the side streets of the wicked quarter mile were not a safe place for a middle class slummer to tread. He was attracting more attention than he felt comfortable with and was worried that he might get robbed, so he moved back out onto the main roads and went off to Commercial Street. It was still early yet, as he had planned to select his prey after 1.00am, when he thought that she would start feeling desperate for a bit of business, as the streets fast emptied of drunk men seeking some female company, in front of her eyes.

Martha had spent most of the night of her murder in the company of a fellow prostitute named Mary Ann Connelly (aka Pearly Poll) and two soldiers. The two women had known each over for about four or five months and for the last few nights Mary had been bedding down in a lodging house in Dorset Street. The group went on a pub-crawl that included a drink or two in the Two Brewers pub on Brick Lane. At 11.45pm Martha and Mary went their separate ways, Martha headed off towards Whitechapel with one of the soldiers and Mary took hers into Angel Alley. At about 12.15am both ladies had concluded their business, but their night's work was not over. The women had had a night out and were well oiled due to the alcohol paid for by the two soldiers, but they still needed to provide their services to other men in order to earn some hard cash to pay their doss. The soldiers had paid for their pleasure with drink and did not part with any cash for the sex that was to follow.

The Ripper had experienced a very stressful night. At first the minutes seemed to pass like hours but now time was passing quickly. There were many whores about but he was not after sex, well not as they would understand it. He was after performing a little surgery and he needed a quiet spot with just enough light to enable him to get his work done. This was going to be more difficult than he'd anticipated as he found himself on the Whitechapel High Street at 12.00am, which allowed him easy access to the alleys and courtyards of the wicked quarter mile. He positioned himself across the road from the White Hart pub, which was on the corner of a narrow alley called George Yard, where he'd noticed the whores leading men from the pub up the alley. The alley was a good spot in terms of privacy, as many smaller alleys and courts led from it.

On concluding her business with the soldier, Martha found herself drunk but short of the 4d needed for her lodgings. She wandered down George Yard onto the Whitechapel High Street. She had no money, so did not venture into the pub, and instead she tried to make herself look presentable and waited on the street corner in the expectation of getting propositioned by one of the drunks leaving the White Hart pub. The Ripper saw her from across the street. It was still early and he was not interested in approaching her just yet as there were too many people about. He was sure that this whore would hang around until the last of the drunks finally left for home. He moved further along the road and planned to return back there in about a quarter of an hour. Closing time was officially 12.30am, but being a bank holiday the pub closed closer to 1.00am. Martha had not been lucky and found herself cold and alone, and was starting to think that she wouldn't get the 4d that would get her a bed for the night. She was walking up the high street when she saw him. There was a toff walking alone on the other side of the street, not rich looking but definitely a slummer. Martha had seen him looking her way and she knew that she had caught his eye. The gent moved off, walking further up the high street. Martha decided to wait for a bit, as she had a feeling that the man would be back and at about 1.15am she saw him again.

No one knows what happened over the next hour or so, but coming up to 2.00am Martha was still out on the streets. It was time for the Ripper to make his move. He met Martha on the Whitechapel High Street, flashing a shilling in front of her to get her attention. The Ripper knew that this was much more than the going rate, but hopefully not too much so as to arouse her suspicions. He was a foreigner, an American, and thought that his unusual accent would give him some leverage with her. He led the whore into George Yard and tried to get her into one of its side alleys. But Martha despite being drunk, smelled a rat, something wasn't quite right with this American toff. He had offered her too much money and now seemed too keen to get her into one of the alleys. Just then a couple passed by, Joseph and Elizabeth Mahoney. They were on their way home to 47 George Yard Buildings, a tenement block occupied by the working poor. Martha saw them enter the block and tried to manoeuvre the Ripper into the doorway. Martha thought that she would be safer there as people were clearly still out and about in the block. However, the Ripper was not keen to go there and after a few minutes he and Martha spied Elizabeth Mahoney leaving the block, she was on her way to Thrawl Street to get some supper from a chandler's shop.

The Ripper was getting agitated, he had waited months for this moment and now it all seemed to be going wrong. He wasn't in control of the situation, the whore was. The

Ripper was angry and agitated and was tempted to leave the whore and find another, but then he calmed down and got back to work. About ten minutes had passed when Elizabeth Mahoney returned to the block with the supper. The stairwell was in darkness, the stairwell lights being extinguished at 11.00pm, but the Ripper had all the light he needed. He noticed that there were no other lights on in the building and felt certain that the couple he'd seen would not venture out again. Martha now felt more comfortable, she was still a bit nervous of this strange American toff, but in a few minutes she'd have earned an easy shilling. She'd then have enough for her night's doss with more than a few pence left over for an ale or a gin. Martha had seen the woman go up the stairs, so she led the Ripper up onto the first floor.

The trap was now set, but it was important for the Ripper to see the look in the whore's eyes when she finally realised that he had her. He gently stroked her head, manoeuvring it into what little light seeped into the landing, and then Martha saw him change from Jekyll into Hyde, but by then it was too late. The Ripper moved at lightning speed, grabbing her around the throat with a strong hand. He smiled as he watched the terror in her eyes as she realised that he meant to kill her. Martha tried to free herself but he was too strong for her. She tried to scream but she couldn't even breathe. Martha passed out and the Ripper placed her on her back on the floor of the landing. He put his left hand over her mouth to ensure that she could not scream and using his right hand plunged the surgeon's knife into her chest. Martha did not feel any pain but the wound was deep and drained the life from her. The whore's capture had gone far from perfectly, but she hadn't made a sound when he attacked her. The Ripper was angry, this was not how it was meant to have been and he went into a frenzy, hacking away at her. He started at her chest, making his way down her torso, finally stabbing her in her stomach, abdomen and vagina. The rage washed over him like a wave and at that moment he was lost to his fantasies. He just stabbed and stabbed again until all the anger evaporated from his mind and body. Then it was over. He did not think that he had much blood on him but in the half-light he could not be sure. He quickly and quietly went back down the stairs into the alley. He wanted to return to the high street but went the other way, staying in the side streets. He knew the location of a stand pump and made his way there to wash away the blood that he thought he might have on his hands and face. He had seen people along the way but nobody took much notice of him, but then what had he done to warrant their attention?

❦ ❦ ❦

Wellcome made his way to Cock Lane, he went down the stairs to the basement and let himself into the warehouse. As he'd expected, nobody else was in the building. He cleaned himself up, changed his clothes and placed the surgical knife back with the others in his collection. He left the warehouse and made his way to Regent's Park and the safety of home. Now as he walked along the streets, he was just another toff out in the early hours of another summer's day.

Martha's body was discovered at 4.50am by a waterside labourer named John Saunders Reeve. Reeve had just left his room at 37 George Yard Buildings to go to work. On seeing a body lying in a pool of blood he ran for a policeman and eventually located a PC Barrett. At 5.30am Dr Timothy Robert Keleene was at the site and examined Martha's body, she had been stabbed 39 times. Dr Keleene was to state that there were no signs of Martha having had a recent connection, meaning that that there was no sign of her having had sexual intercourse. So neither the soldier nor the Ripper had had full intercourse with her. Dr

Keleene added that there was a great deal of blood between her legs, which had been separated.

I have included two maps with information about the murder locations. The first provides an overview of all the Whitechapel murder sites, together with their proximity to the Burroughs Wellcome and Co warehouse in Cock Lane. The second is a local map showing George Yard and the site of the Tabram murder. Although far from conclusive, the first map does appear to show that the Whitechapel murders were committed by a man that may have come from the direction of Newgate Street.

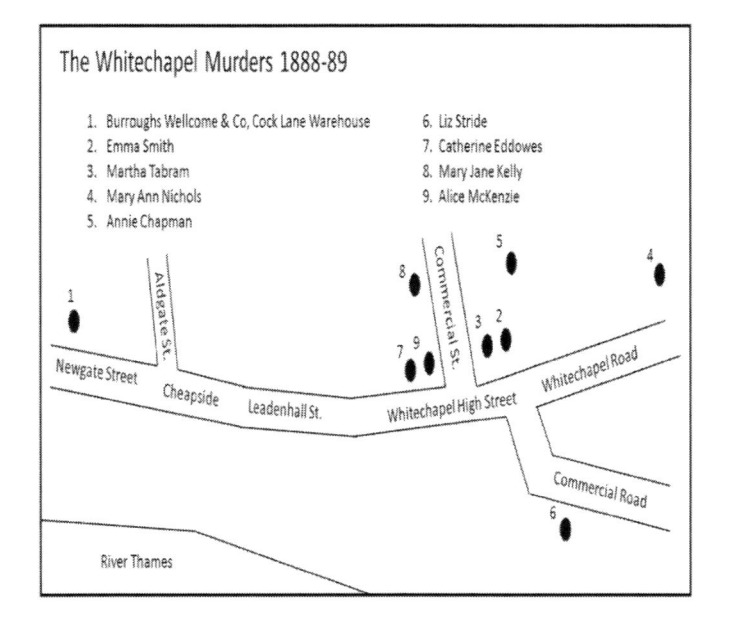

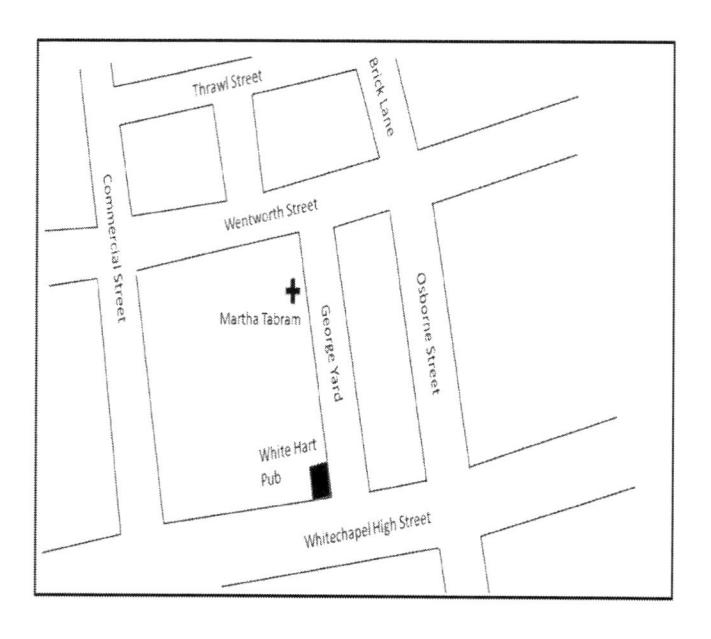

CHAPTER TEN

The Police – A Slow Start

In 1888, the Metropolitan Police district was spilt into 21 Divisions, each allocated a capital letter. The area named Stepney (which included Whitechapel) came under H Division. Police Officers in H Division were numbered upwards from one with the suffix H., with police constable H. Barrett, the first police office to arrive at the scene of Martha Tabram's murder being numbered 226H. However, only three of the five murders attributed to Jack the Ripper were committed within the boundary of H Division, with one murder committed in Bethnal Green (J Division) and another in the jurisdiction of the City Police.

The most senior officer of the Met in 1888 was Sir Charles Warren, who started life in his new role back in 1886 by instructing his men to deal with any social or political disturbances with a heavy hand. And so in November of 1887, a year known for its bad weather and particularly high unemployment, his men dealt with a peaceful demonstration in London's Trafalgar Square in paramilitary fashion. The press, and in particular the Star newspaper, did not take kindly to this new fashion of policing and were highly critical of Sir Charles and his force. This did not bode well for his new career and in 1888 things were to go from bad to worse.

Emma Smith had been murdered in Whitechapel over the April bank holiday weekend. Her death was brutal even by Whitechapel standards but did not warrant any special investigation by the officers of H Division. The officer tasked with leading the investigation into her death was Inspector Edmund John James Reid. Reid was born 1846 and joined the Met in back in 1872. He was a respected and successful investigator and had succeeded an equally respected Inspector by the name of Frederick George Abberline as head of H Division CID in 1888. Reid was no ordinary man and was known to make balloon ascents and parachute jumps in his leisure time, and even received a medal for setting a high altitude record. Not much is recorded about Smith's death, but a police report of Reid's still exists in which he wrote 'The peritoneum had been penetrated by a blunt instrument thrust up the woman's passage, and peritonitis set in which caused death. She was aged 45 years, 5ft 2in. high, complexion fair, hair light brown, scar on right temple. No description of men'. Reid was involved in the Whitechapel murders from the very beginning, but the Ripper was not aware of a policeman like Reid and or cared nothing for his existence.

Reid is a fine example of the quality of men involved in trying to solve the Whitechapel murders. In the main, the detectives involved with the case were clever, diligent, hard-working men. However, for all their commitment and skill, they belonged to a pre-serial killer age in which the perpetrators of offences were deemed to have a logical motive for their actions. Detectives like Reid were soon to find that all their knowledge, insight and experience were to count for nothing when trying to investigate the apparently motiveless crimes of Jack the Ripper.

Whatever the inadequacies of the detectives and other officers on the ground, it was the actions of the men at the top of the police force that were going to set the tone for the whole investigation. Soon after taking charge, Sir Charles experienced problems with his relationship with his Deputy Commissioner, James Monroe, and their differences culminated in Monroe's resignation in July 1888. His replacement, Dr Robert Anderson, whose responsibilities included heading-up the CID, was on the verge of taking sick leave when he started in his new post on 1 September 1888. Sir Charles had already booked his annual leave for September in order that he might return refreshed for duty for what he expected to be the start of the political demonstration season in October, and he instructed his new number two to do the same. Therefore on Saturday 1 September, the day on which Mary Ann Nichols was found murdered, Sir Charles was on holiday in the South of France, and would be followed a week later by Dr Anderson, who on medical advice left the country for a month's break in Switzerland. Therefore, just as the police force began to realise that they were dealing with a serial murderer, in what was to become the most famous murder case the world has ever known, the Commissioner and Deputy Commissioner of the Metropolitan Police were out of the country on their respective holidays and sick leave.

Just as in the case of Emma Smith, Inspector Reid was assigned to investigate Martha Tabram's murder. In a report dated 6 August, Reid described how Martha's body had been identified, that a statement had been taken from her friend Pearly Poll, and that it had not yet proved possible to identify the two soldiers the women had been out drinking with. His report ended, as might be expected, stating that inquiries into the murder were ongoing. So for all Reid's efforts, no motive or suspect had been identified for either of the two violent murders committed on the two Whitechapel prostitutes.

The investigation into the Whitechapel murders was highly criticised by the press, although this may have had more to do with the media's relationship with Sir Charles Warren rather than the force as a whole. However, over the passage of time, the police have not fared favourably with Ripperologists either, with much criticism levelled at them for the ineffectual cross-referencing of leads and for the misspelling of suspects' and witnesses' names. However, it must be remembered that in the late eighteenth century there were no computers with massive databases to be analysed by data-mining professionals, no DNA, no

CCTV, nor even finger printing technology; so it is likely that the police did as well as might be expected of them. That said, any police incompetence made for good news copy and as already mentioned, the absence of the two men at the top of the organisation, made the police an easy target for editors with newspapers to sell.

Reid wrote in one of his reports, that Mary Ann Connelly came forward and provided the police with a statement to the effect that she and Martha Tabram had spent the night in the company of two soldiers but didn't know their names or the names of their regiments. However, she did remember them having white bands around their caps, which indicated that they were members of the Coldstream Guards, based at the Wellington Barracks. Reid personally supervised several line-ups of soldiers taken from Wellington Barracks who had been on leave on the night of the murder. On a line-up arranged for 15th August, Connelly unhesitatingly picked out two men, privates George and Skipper. Not that it really mattered to the overall investigation but both men were able to provide alibis for the night of the murder, greatly reducing Connelly's credibility as a reliable witness. Reid fared little better with the George Yard beat officer, PC Barrett, who also picked out another two soldiers who were able to produce cast-iron alibis for their whereabouts on the night of the murder. Reid was to write that 'enquiries were made to find some other person who saw the deceased and Pearly Poll with the privates on the night of the 6th but without success, and Pearly Poll and the P.C. having both picked out the wrong men they could not by trusted again as their evidence would be worthless'. So, with no other leads to follow, the investigation quickly fizzled out.

The inquest into Martha's death was held on 9 August at the Working Lad's Institute, Whitechapel Road. The inquest was presided over by the deputy coroner, George Collier, who was standing in for the coroner, Wynne E.

Baxter, who was on holiday. There was still some uncertainty over Martha's identity, so a decision was made to adjourn the inquest in order to allow more time for a formal identification of the body. The inquest was reopened two weeks later, more evidence was heard but proceedings took place quickly and the jury soon returned the now infamous verdict of 'wilful murder against some person or persons unknown'.

The murder of Martha Tabram provides us with an insight into the life of London's eighteenth century poor. She had been brutally murdered, stabbed 39 times, but interest in her death was minimal with few people outside of the police and other public officials being present at the inquest. This apparent lack of interest was both good and bad for a serial murderer like the Ripper. One one hand it was good, in that the lack of publicity would most likely result in the whores of Whitechapel keeping down their guards, making them easy pickings for any future attack. On the other hand it was bad, in that he had fewer objects to help him relive the fantasy of the murder. Reading about or hearing from others about the details of Tabram's demise would have brought back to him some feelings of the excitement he'd have felt when he had captured and killed her, the lack of such news would have left him feeling frustrated and empty.

Such feelings are 'normal' to any serial killer. As the excitement faded, the Ripper would have entered the totem phase shortly after Martha's death and the depression phase a few days after that. A lot of serial killers relive the excitement of their evil acts by taking a trophy (an item of clothing, jewellery or even a body part) from their victims. It is not thought that the Ripper took a trophy from Martha Tabram; he would not be so remiss with his future victims.

It is likely that the Ripper had only scratched the surface of his fantasies in his first fumbled murder. He wanted to feel the sexual urges that the performance of surgery gave him, the feelings he had experienced as a young boy, when he'd watched his uncle working on the semi-naked women savaged at the hands of the Indians of the frontier. He needed to kill again, and soon. Next time he would take more control over the theatre of murder. For all his planning, he had let the whore led him onto a stairwell and even in his fantasy fuelled frenzy, he dared not slice her up in such a confined public place. Next time would be different.

Although my interest lies in the life of Henry Wellcome, I found what I thought to be an interesting aside to the Martha Tabram investigation. As in addition to the likes of Detective Inspector Reid, another officer involved in the investigation of her murder was Charles H. Cutbush. Cutbush was the author of several 'Special Reports' making reference to Tabram's murder which were addressed directly to the Assistant Commissioner of the CID. What I found interesting was that Mr Cutbush's nephew; a man named Thomas Cutbush, would one day be placed in a lunatic asylum for attacking and stabbing women with knives. Now it is possible that Charles Cutbush knew nothing of his nephew's mental state, but eventually the link was found and articles started appearing in the Sun newspaper hinting that Thomas Cutbush could have been the Ripper. The newspaper quite rightly took the stance that it thought it very unusual that a man like Thomas Cutbush had managed to slip through the police net back in 1888, with no mention of his being a potential suspect throughout the entire Whitechapel murder investigation. The implication was that the Metropolitan Police had put the interests of its own reputation above that of bringing the killer to justice, with it not wishing to admit to any possible link between the serial murderer and one of its officers. I have expanded upon this in the appendix, where details of the main Ripper suspects are summarised.

It is not obvious, since the method of each killing was

different, why the police decided to link the gruesome murders of the three Whitechapel prostitutes which occurred over a five-month period in 1888, especially since the first (Emma Smith's) had been put down to one of the many London Street gangs. Nevertheless they did and so began the makings of a legend.

CHAPTER ELEVEN

Mary Ann Nichols – The Makings of a Surgeon

Mary Ann Nichols (nee Walker), aka Polly Nichols had just turned 43 on the night of her murder, being born on 26th August 1845. She was about 5ft 2in. tall, with dark brown greying hair, brown eyes and was missing about three teeth. Polly as she liked to be called was the second of three children born in Shoe Lane, just off Fleet Street in London. Her early life was not mired with tragedy like that of Martha Tabram. Her father Edward worked as a locksmith and a blacksmith and his wife Caroline as a laundress. Polly married an Oxford born printer, William Nichols, on 16 January 1864. Unfortunately, the marriage was not a happy one with Polly and Edward separating in 1880. As was the case with Martha Tabram, drink played its part in the break-up of yet another marriage. It is known that Polly spent a lot of time in London's workhouses between 1880 and 1888. In the last few weeks of her life, she slept at dosshouses in Thrawl Street and Flower and Dean Street.

※ ※ ※

The Ripper was back in the trolling phase. This time he decided to choose his location in advance and stick to it. The last whore had given the Ripper trouble, as she wouldn't go into one of the deserted little back alleys with him. This had forced him to kill her on the stairwell of a residential block of dwellings, severely restricting what he could do to the body. Yes, he wouldn't let that happen again. At the very far end of Whitechapel he found a quiet residential street, Buck's Row (now named Durward Street).

It ran from west to east between Brady Street and Baker's Row (now Vallance Street), running parallel to the London and North Eastern Railway line. Two narrow bridge roads ran off it both leading onto the Whitechapel Road. Buck's Row contained a number of warehouses, one of which belonged to the company Messrs Kearley and Tonge Limited. During the day, Buck's Row was a busy place but in the dead of the night, it was dark, deserted and a street where people tended to keep themselves to themselves.

The night of Thursday 30 August was cloudy and a storm was brewing, so the Ripper expected not to attract any undue attention in his dark raincoat. He planned to use the same routine as used for his first kill, with a change of clothes waiting from him back at the warehouse. This time he decided to steer clear of the wicked quarter mile, he would stay on the main roads where he felt safer. At 11.00pm he found himself back on the Whitechapel Road. There were a lot of people about and a number of whores were vying for his attention.

On the last night of her life, Polly Nichols had the choice of spending what money she had on her doss or on gin, rum and ale. She did as she always did and decided to go out and have a few drinks, hoping that she would earn back her doss money before the night was out. It was an awful summer night with frequent rain and bouts of thunder and lightning. Polly found herself drinking alone in the Frying Pan pub on Brick Lane, which she left at closing time. She'd been over confident and for whatever reason, probably due to the inclement weather, she had not earned the four pence that would have gotten her a bed for the night. So, being wet, cold, drunk and penniless she tried to blag a night at a dosshouse at number 18 Thrawl Street, where she had stayed the night between the second and twentyfourth of August. She was by now a familiar face and so had no trouble in gaining access to the lodging house, but at 1.20am the deputy lodging-house keeper asked Polly to stump up the 4d for her doss. Polly did not have it and her recent custom counted for nothing as the deputy promptly turned her back out onto street on that rain sodden night. Polly seemed unconcerned by this and left laughing, saying that she would soon get her doss money now that she had a new black bonnet and happily went on her way.

At 2.30am Polly bumped into a friend of hers, Emily Holland. Emily had been down to the river to see a huge fire that had been blazing at the Ratcliffe Docks. As chance would have it, Emily was now on her way to 18 Thrawl Street and as the two women had previously shared a room there, she tried to persuade Polly to return back there with her. Polly refused, saying something about making and spending her doss money three times over earlier that night and went on her way, staggering down the Whitechapel Road.

The Ripper had chosen the venue for his intended assault; all that was needed now was a willing victim, who he hoped to entice off the Whitechapel Road. He had his eye on a whore whom he thought looked particularly desperate to earn a little money. He had planned to ensnare a whore close to 3.15am, the same time that PC John Thain , office number 96J, started making his way down Buck's Row. The Ripper's planning had not been in vain and he approached the whore exactly as PC Thain approached Buck's Row, walking at his regulation 2.5 miles per hour.

The Ripper was in the wooing stage, and so was being as charming as his blood lust would allow. He wanted to slaughter the whore as soon as he had approached her, but he knew he could not attack her out on the main road. Polly was by now beginning to sober-up, she was tired and was keen to get her doss money and go back to Thrawl Street, where her friend Emily had already bedded down for the night. The couple entered Buck's Row from Baker's Row, passed the Kearley and Tonge warehouses and followed the road until it forked. They took the left fork close to the Boarding School. It was near perfect spot; exposed but dark, quiet and deserted. The woman seemed a little nervous but he could tell that she felt on safe ground, being on a residential street. Then he went into capture mode and was on her in a split second, grabbing her around the throat. Polly wanted to scream, but just like Martha Tabram before her, she could not even draw a breath. Again the Ripper wanted to see the terror in the whore's eyes at the moment when it finally dawned upon her that she was about to die. Polly passed out before his eyes and he laid her gently on her back and quickly got on with his work. This time he would do the job right. He took the surgeon's knife and cut into her throat, making two deep wounds, the first through the left carotid artery. The blood of a fully conscious person would have spurted everywhere, but the heart of the half throttled whore was barely beating and the blood oozed slowly from the incisions in her neck. He toyed with taking her head clean off, but the knife was not up to the job. He stabbed at the vertebrate in her neck, but without success. Then for a few minutes he was lost in his fantasies. He lifted the whore's skirts and he started playing his little games. He sliced into her, just like he remembered his uncle doing back when he was a boy.

When it was over and the Ripper returned to reality, he remembered how empty he had felt shortly after killing the last victim. He wanted something to remember this one by, something that would help him relive the moment. He noticed that she had a ring on her middle finger. His hands were wet with blood, so he took a cloth from his pocket and cleaned himself up. Then he pulled the ring from her finger, placed it in a pouch and slipped it into his pocket. He looked up and down the dark narrow road to check that the coast was clear and then he took off into the night. He made his way to a standpipe that he had seen the week before and washed the rest of the blood from his face and hands. Then he made his way quickly to the basement warehouse. Once inside he was safe again. He changed his clothes, being careful to remember to remove the whore's ring from the pocket. He replaced the knife back in his collection of curios and went off out in time to witness the sun rising over what would turn out to be a fine summer's day.

※ ※ ※

Polly's body was found shortly after the Ripper left the crime scene. At 3.45am Charles Cross walked in to Buck's Row and saw a shape that he thought might be a woman lying against the gates of the stables. He was deciding what to do when another man entered the road. At first Robert Paul thought that the man loitering in the darkness was going attack him. However, he believed the man when he told him that there was a woman lying on the floor. The two men went over to the woman and Cross felt her hands, they were already cold and limp. Paul felt her face, it was still warm and he thought that he heard her breathing. Paul wanted to move the woman, but Cross refused; he said that he was late for work and couldn't waste anymore of his time on her. The two men not realising the extent of Polly's injuries, agreed to carry on with their journeys to their respective workplaces and only report the incident, should they happen to meet a passing police officer along the way. The actions of these men provide a classic example of what life was like in the Rookeries, where the discovery of a dead or dying woman took second place to ensuring that they weren't late into work.

As the two men left Buck's Row, PC Neil, officer number 97J, entered the Row from Brady Street and discovered Polly lying on the pavement. Her body was still warm, but she was clearly past saving, as the last of her life slowly drained from her body, along with her blood that was now flowing along the gutter.

Even though Polly's murder was different to Martha's, in that her throat had been cut and that she had been 'ripped-up' as opposed to stabbed, the police concluded that the same hand was responsible for both women's deaths. Polly's murder had taken place in the Met's J Division, so it fell to new officers, Inspectors Spratling and Helson to take the case forward. Inspector Reid would have been made aware of the details of the murder but it was up to his J Division colleagues to follow-up on any leads. In a report dated 7 September, Inspector Helson wrote that a man named Jack Pizer, aka Leather Apron, was known to have been ill-using prostitutes for a considerable period of time. He added that a careful search was underway to try and find him.

So it appeared that J Division were making more progress than their colleagues in H Division, as the police now had the name of a suspect. Conventional theory had it that the motives behind the murders were simple, so the confidence of the police officers would now have been high that they might now have identified the killer.

Given below is a plan showing the site of Polly Nichol's murder and its location close to the Whitechapel Road and London Hospital.

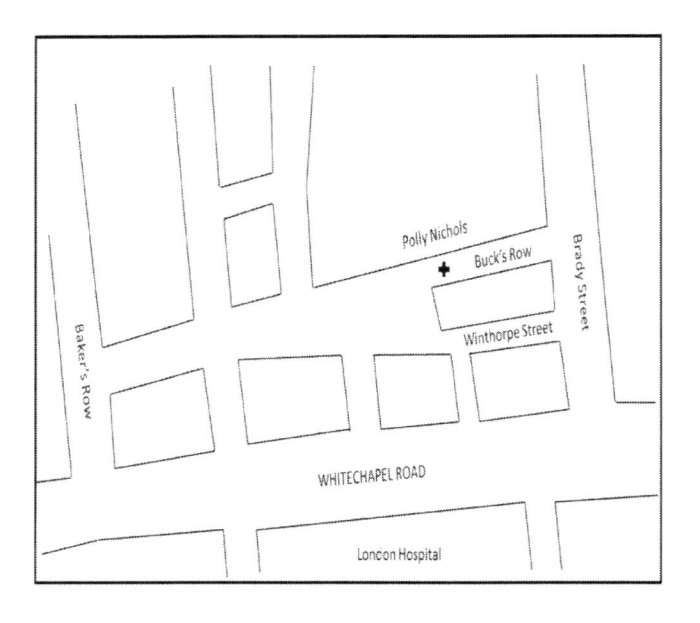

CHAPTER TWELVE

The Press – Before the Ripper

If newspapers had not existed in the 19th century it is unlikely that you would have found yourself in the 21st century reading about a series of murders that occurred in and around Whitechapel back in 1888. In the early days newspapers were for the gentry, the mass of the populace either being unable to read or unable to afford to buy them. The situation was not helped by the introduction of the Stamp Act, which was a tax imposed upon British newspapers in 1712. At its height, the duty on newspapers reached 4d, the cost of a bed for the night in a common lodging house, placing them beyond the means of the masses. Over time the level of literacy slowly improved and the demand for newspapers increased. In 1855 London had ten newspapers, including the Daily Telegraph, which was launched a few days before the repeal of the Stamp Act on 29 June of that year. The most expensive newspaper was the Times, costing 7d. Despite the high levels of illiteracy in the general population the Times had a circulation in excess of 10,000 copies a day. Seeing the opportunity to take the lead in an expanding market, the owner of the Telegraph dropped its price to a penny, making it the first 1d morning newspaper. Within a year the Telegraph's morning paper was selling in excess of 27,000 copies a day. By the 1880s, the press, following the lead of the Pall Mall Gazette, were producing stories based upon a very successful mixture of sensationalism and social investigation. No doubt, the editor of the PMG (W.T. Stead) would have been proud of the newspaper's sensationalist reporting of the fate of the Titanic, with whose sinking he met his death.

The competition amongst publications forced their prices down, but with this came the need for headline grabbing stories to increase sales. By the time of Mary Ann Nichol's gruesome death, the press realised that they had the makings of a long running story. The police had done some of the headline writers' jobs for them in linking the three murders of Nichols, Tabram and Smith together under the umbrella of the 'Whitechapel Murders'. The headlines read, 'Another Horrible Murder in Whitechapel' or as the street vendors called them 'Nother orrible murder. Get yer paper ere'. However, the press were soon to get a much better headline, one that would sell newspapers and books for well over a hundred years.

The Daily Telegraph ran a long article on page three, with extensive details of the inquest into Nichol's death. The story made reference to the body being 'nearly drained of blood', adding that 'The police have no theory with respect to the matter, except that a sort of "High Rip" gang exists in the neighbourhood'. So the Telegraph article implies that Nichol's might have actually been murdered elsewhere due to the lack of blood at the scene of the murder. Also, the paper knew that a gang were suspected of murdering Emma Smith back in April, so needing a suspect to capture the public's imagination, they made one up.

The newspapers maintained a running commentary of the inquest into Nichol's death. The first session started on Saturday 3 September, with the first newspaper reports published from Monday 5 September.

CHAPTER THIRTEEN

Business as Usual

In the midst of the mayhem being caused by the Ripper, it was business as usual for Burroughs Wellcome and Co. The company had ended its relationship with one of its two early stakeholders McKesson & Robbins in 1886, no longer selling on the company's tablets. However, a dispute over trademarks continued through most of 1887, with Rhodes James noting that McK & R had informed its clients that they had abandoned their relationship with Burroughs Wellcome; the implication being that McK & R no longer wanted to be associated with Burroughs Wellcome & Company's products.

1888 was the year that Burroughs Wellcome decided to free itself from its other stakeholder, John Wyeth & Brother. Of the two companies, it appears that McK & R produced higher quality products, with Wellcome never having been happy with the quality of the pills produced by Wyeth's. In 1888 Wyeth's machines were not as good as their competitors, with pills produced from them being more expensive and of lower quality than others on the market. Staff at Burroughs Wellcome had been busy trying to make their own improvements to Wyeth's machines in a bid to improve the quality of their products. Matters came to a head when Wyeth refused to let Burroughs Wellcome use these new improved machines. So in the midst of the Ripper killing spree, Wellcome wrote to Wyeth on 5 September 1888 offering to sell the company improved versions of their own machines. Wyeth's response to Wellcome's letter is predictable, stating that the company had decided to terminate its long-standing contract. The company that had helped Burroughs Wellcome & Co establish itself in the market of compressed medicines had suffered the indignity of the servant offering the master an improved product; something they were never going to be happy accepting.

This left Burroughs Wellcome & Co free to do business as they pleased. They were now manufacturing their own products, with brand new fully automated machines and were finally free from commission payments to their partner organisations. There was an inherent risk in breaking ties from their partners, in that the company's future would now be dependent solely on the quality of their own products. However, the future looked very bright for the owners of this now self-reliant company.

Wellcome's battle with Burroughs was relentless. Rhodes James informs that Wellcome received a letter dated 4 September 1888 from his brother George, in which George wrote of being astonished to hear of the trouble his brother had been going through, adding that he hoped that Burroughs would come to justice in the end. George was no doubt responding to a letter that he or another family member must have recently received from Henry. Such correspondence proves that Henry Wellcome was under massive strain in August 1888 and that the pressure was beginning to tell. His battle with Burroughs had started in 1887 and was now at its most intense. Wellcome had spent the last year watching his reputation and financial resources slowly being eaten away and in August 1888 it seems that he was not sure that he would be able to weather the storm. He appears to have become ground down physically and fallen into a form of despair. All this fits well with the theory that external stressors push potential serial killers over the edge; into the realms of madness and murder. I think that George's letter shows us that if Henry Wellcome had the potential to become a severely socially dysfunctional individual, then August 1888 was the month that he might well have fallen into the abyss.

CHAPTER FOURTEEN

Annie Chapman – Another Curio for the Collection

Mary Ann Nichols was buried on the afternoon of Thursday 6 September and it didn't take long for things to start getting back to normal in the wicked quarter mile. The fallen women were always at the mercy of the street gangs, but having three of their number being killed by the same gang was something that nobody had ever heard of before. However, the laws of probability might have been at work, there being thousands of prostitutes in Whitechapel, and so the fallen women may have thought that it was only a matter of time before something like this happened to some of their number. The odds of being killed now seemed much lower than before but that wasn't likely to stop these women getting out and trying to earn their doss money. It was a classic case of Catch 22, if the women didn't get their doss they would have to sleep on the streets, but if they were on the streets they were at the mercy of the gangs. There wasn't anything for it, the unfortunates of Whitechapel would have to continue earning their livelihoods in the same way that some women had been forced into doing over the millennia.

Annie Eliza Chapman (nee Smith), aka Annie Siffey was soon to be 47 or 48 years old (it not being certain if she was born in September 1840 or 1841). She was about 5ft tall, with dark brown wavy hair, a dark complexion, blue eyes and was missing several teeth. Annie was a Londoner, the first of five children most likely born in the district of Paddington. Her family left London for Clewer in Somerset when Annie was about 21 years old but she stayed behind and may have worked as a domestic servant in order to make ends meet. She married John Chapman, a gentleman's coachman, on 1 May 1869 at All Saints Church in the district of Knightsbridge. The couple had two children and in 1873 were living at 17 South Bruton Mews in London, an area that provided stables for the well-heeled residents of Berkeley Square. Things must have gradually taken a turn for the worse as in 1880 Annie and her family followed her parents from London to Clewer, living in the attic rooms of St Leonard's Hill Farm Cottage. Annie was drinking heavily and had even been held by the police for drunkenness when her first child was only ten years old. The marriage finally broke-up and the couple separated around the year 1882. Annie moved back to London and would have been able to make ends meet because John was paying her a weekly allowance of 10 shillings a week. However, on Christmas Day 1886 John Chapman died and Annie's support money was no more. From this time onwards Annie was forced to live in common lodging houses in and around the wicked quarter mile. By 1888 she was having a relationship with a retired soldier named Edward Stanley. Ted Stanley was also known as 'The Pensioner' because he had a small army pension. However, Stanley was no knight in shining armour and only paid for Annie's bed when they shared one together. On the nights that they weren't together Annie had to find her doss money by any means available to her.

In the week before her death, Annie Chapman had gotten into a fight with woman in a local pub called The Britannia. The Britannia, known locally by the landlord's surname, the Ringers, was located on the corner of Dorset and Commercial Streets. The fight left Annie badly shaken, with a black eye and bruising to her chest. On Tuesday 4 September a friend of Annie's named Amelia Farmer met the bedraggled looking Chapman wandering the streets close to the Spitalfields Church. Annie told Amelia that she was ill and that she thought she needed to spend a day or two in the casual ward. Amelia could see that Annie wasn't in a fit state to 'earn' any money for food, let alone her doss. So even though she had hardly a penny to her name, Amelia gave Annie 2d (half a night's doss money) and asked her to try not to spend it on rum.

Annie's whereabouts are unknown from the time of her meeting with Amelia Farmer on that Tuesday until she appeared at her regular dosshouse, at 35 Dorset Street, on Friday 7 September. She arrived there between 2pm and 3pm bumping into the warden, Tim Donovan, on her arrival. She asked Donovan if she could use the kitchen and since he knew her to be a regular, Donovan allowed her into the building. Annie left the dosshouse a few hours later and again met her friend Amelia whilst wandering the streets. Amelia asked Annie if she was going to Stratford that day to try and sell a few trinkets, which Amelia knew to be Annie's main source of legitimate income. Annie told her that she was too ill for that, but after about ten minutes she said that it was no use her giving way to illness; Amelia remembered her specifically saying that 'I must pull myself together and go and get some money, or I shall have no lodgings'. So in the early evening of Friday 7 September, the unwell Annie Chapman forced herself to walk the streets of Whitechapel in the hope of making enough money for a bed for the night. Any extra money for the likes of food would have been a bonus to her.

Annie was ill, but she had heard of all the talk about the murders. She thought that they might be the work of a street gang who frequented the Whitechapel Road, so she kept well away from there, staying close to Brick Lane, the top end of Commercial Street and the area around the Spitalfields market. She had been lucky, she had found a punter or two and had made her doss money but she was still starving and really felt like a drink. She had been given some medicine at the casual ward, a couple bottles containing tonics and a few pills in a box. She didn't really trust the pills, so had not touched them. Then at about midnight she went back to 35 Dorset Street and did not have any trouble getting back into the building, as she'd been there earlier in the day. She was knackered and asked if someone would fetch her a beer from the local pub. At 12.30am Annie supped a pint with William Stevens, a painter by trade. Annie told Stevens that she had spent the last few days in the casual ward. He noticed that she had two bottles of medicine and a box containing two pills. Annie was fidgeting with the box and it fell to pieces, so she placed the pills into envelope that she found on the floor and shoved it inside her pocket. Annie had chosen alcohol over a bed for the night and now did not have her doss money. So refreshed by the beer, she headed back out into the night in the expectation of earning some more money.

Annie was out of luck, she hadn't found herself a punter after the pubs had turned their customers out for the night, so she returned to the dosshouse at about 1.45am. Having no money and hoping for a freebie, she headed straight down to the kitchen. However, Tim Donovan, the warden, saw her go and sent the night watchman to get payment from her. Annie tended to sleep in a double bunk, alone or with her male friend Ted Stanley, so she was asked to pay 8d for the night. Annie returned to the office and informed Donovan that she didn't have the money for her bed and as she might have expected, Donovan told her that she would have to leave the building. Annie liked sleeping in her regular bunk and asked Donovan to hold it for her, telling him that she would soon be back with the money and headed off back out into the night.

✟ ✟ ✟

The Ripper was now getting familiar with the streets of Whitechapel. He knew that the area around the market was pretty much deserted after 1.30am and would remain so until about 5.00am. Annie had had a few pints, but she was sober enough to be afraid to tout her wares on the Whitechapel Road, so she stayed close to the Spitalfield market. The time passed slowly and after a few hours she lost all hope of earning her doss money. It was early September, so she hoped that Saturday would be warm and that she could find somewhere to sleep when it got light. There wasn't anything else for her to do, she would have to keep on the move until the morning light.

The Ripper had not bothered to venture out early that night. It was gone 2.00am before he set-off for Whitechapel. London was a 24 hour city, but he was surprised by the number of people he saw on the streets. He was in Whitechapel by 3.00am and took a walk along Hanbury Street, which was surprisingly empty, without a whore to be seen. He decided to stay close to the main thoroughfare, Commercial Street, but was back in Hanbury Street at close to 4.00am. The nearby Ten Bells pub was open on account of its special licence, but the streets were still pretty much deserted. Then he saw a whore in the distance and followed her down the road. His blood was racing now, he was very much back in the wooing phase and wanted to make contact with his chosen prey. Then just as he was about to make his move, a man came out of nowhere and soon the gent and the whore went off to a secluded spot for a bit of business. The Ripper decided to take another walk around the block. Time now began to pass more rapidly, the quarter hour chimes of church bells seeming to run continuously in his mind. Just as he was thinking that he had made a mistake and had left it too late, he saw her. Yes, the dishevelled little woman would be perfect. She was heading in the direction of Hanbury Street and he felt confident of being able to persuade her into accompanying him into the backyard of number 29.

Annie was dog tired when she saw the Ripper. She wasn't afraid of him and he certainly did not have the appearance of a gang member. He gave her a friendly smile and bade her a good morning, letting her know that he was up for a little business.

The Ripper manoeuvred the whore into Hanbury Street, just as the Spitalfields' church bell chimed the quarter hour at 5.15am. He was hoping that the whore would lead him into the backyard of number 29 and she did not disappoint. Annie had used the yard many times before and she led her punter through the corridor to the back of the building. She opened the back door, it was quite dark but she knew to expect the three steps that lead down into the yard. The moment of the kill was almost upon them and the Ripper almost lost control with the excitement. Just then he heard sounds from over the fence, someone was walking around in the adjacent garden. A carpenter named Albert Cadosch had gone to use the outside toilet in the yard of 27 Hanbury Street. Albert heard voices over the fence as he returned back into the warmth of the house, but hearing the sound of people in the backyard of number 29 wasn't anything unusual, so he didn't give it another thought.

The Ripper could not wait any longer and set on Annie in a flash. He had heard the person re-enter the house and did not know when someone else might access the yard. He grabbed Annie around the throat and smiled as he throttled the life out of her. Again, he wanted to see the fear in the whore's eyes and she did not disappoint him. He held her against the fence and she passed out before his eyes. He had experienced the thrill in capturing his prey and now wanted to enact his murderous fantasies. He was just about to set to work when the next door's yard door opened again. The Ripper did not panic and he carefully lowered the whore to the floor. He could tell that someone had gone to use the outside toilet, so he decided not to cut the whore just yet. He kept himself busy by wrenching the rings from her fingers and rifling through her pockets. After what seemed like an age, he finally heard the person re-enter the house for the second time. He then set to work as quickly and quietly as he could. He sliced into the whore's body just like the surgeon of his dreams. This time he would throw her entrails over her shoulder, as in the punishment metered out by the Brotherhood to those who had committed crimes against humanity. He had not cut Annie's intestines clean through, so her entrails were still attached to her body when he threw them over her right-shoulder. He thought that they looked like string around her neck and gave the appearance of a necklace, with the blood glistening from them in the half light of the yard. Before he was finished, he cut away her belly button and her uterus. He planned to store these in jars using some preserving fluid. He looked down at the whore, she was on her back, her legs bent and apart, with her skirts raised over her knees. He was not sure why, but he decided to lift her left arm over her body, covering the hole he had made inside of her.

Then it was over, he had finished his work and normal thoughts began entering his mind and he suddenly realised that he was in serious danger of being caught. There was a washbasin in the yard but he did not have to time to use it. The sun was starting to rise in the sky and he had to hope that it would stay dark long enough for him to get back to the warehouse before people would be able to notice the blood on him. The Ripper opened the back door of the house, quietly walked the length of the passage, opened the front door and went off into the dawn of a new day.

※ ※ ※

John Davis woke to the sound of the Spitalfields' church bell chiming the quarter hour that denoted that it was 5.45am. He made himself a cup of tea and then went downstairs with the intention of using the outside toilet that was located in the backyard. When he entered the passage he noticed that the front door had been left wide open. He walked along the passage to the backyard and immediately saw the body upon opening the back door.

The following map shows the vicinity of the Chapman murder scene relative to the Christ Church, Spitalfields market and Ten Bells pub.

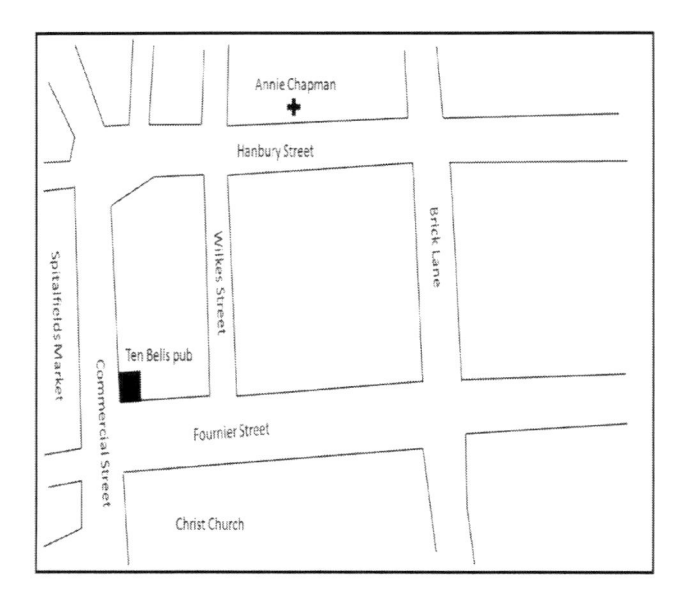

CHAPTER FIFTEEN

Loss of Faith and the Creation of the Whitechapel Vigilance Committee

Chapman's murder led to an explosion of emotion in Whitechapel. Thousands of people came out onto the streets to find out more about the killing. Large crowds waited around the newsstands until the latest editions came in, so as to get the latest information about the murder.

The police had not caught the killer or killers, but were about to get their best lead yet. At 7am a strange, frightening looking man entered the Prince Albert pub on Brushfield Street, better known at the time as the Clean House. The pub was around the corner from Hanbury Street. The man asked the landlady, Mrs Fiddymont, for a half pint of ale, which she was unhappy to furnish him with, whilst being careful not to look the man directly in the eye. In the exchange she noticed that her frightening looking customer had blood on the back of his right hand and between his fingers. She studied him further through the mirror in the back of the bar and noticed that he was wearing a light-blue checked shirt, torn on his right shoulder and had a narrow streak of blood under his right ear. Then, the man suddenly becoming aware of Mrs Fiddymont observing him in the mirror, gulped down his ale and left the pub. A few locals followed him outside, with one of their number, a man named Joseph Taylor being brave enough to walk alongside of him. Taylor was later to describe the man as being of slim build, about 5 feet 8 inches in height, with a ginger coloured moustache, short sandy hair and wild eyes, like a hawk's. There were other witness statements with details of another man seen with a woman outside of 29 Hanbury Street at about 5.30am, but it appears that the police were much more interested in trying to identify Mrs Fiddymont's mystery stranger. Fortunately for Henry Wellcome, a description of a 5ft 8in. tall man with a ginger coloured moustache was never passed onto the press.

The police now turned their attention away from street gangs and it was proposed that the murders might be the work of a lone killer. It is not clear why the press were not given the description of the ginger moustached man with the hawk's eyes, so lacking that information, they only published the witness statement that described the man seen in Hanbury Street as 5.30am. He was described as 'foreign' looking and standing about feet 8 inches in height. So in effect, the press were now warning Whitechapel's fallen woman to be wary of lone men, but not just any type of lone male, no they should be on the lookout for a foreigner or more specifically, a man of Jewish appearance.

Chapman's murder took place back in Whitechapel, so H Division was back in the driving seat. Inspector Reid had been on annual leave when the murder was committed and on his return to work found that changes had been made to the running of the investigation. The press coverage had resulted in the senior ranks of the Met setting up a special Whitechapel Murder Unit that would control action across the different police divisions. Reid found himself reporting to the man that he had replaced back in 1887, as Frederick George Abberline had been reassigned from his duties at Scotland Yard to co-ordinate the efforts of the detectives.

Inspector Abberline was born in 1843, he was a portly man who supposedly gave the appearance of being a bank manager or solicitor, rather than a detective inspector, first class. He joined the Met in 1863 and was H Division's Local Inspector from 1878 to 1887. Over that time he gained unrivalled knowledge of the East End and its criminals. He was an excellent detective and in 1887 had been transferred to Scotland Yard under the recommendation of the then Assistant Commissioner, James Monro. Over the months that followed his reassignment to the investigation, Abberline would be Scotland Yard's man on the ground and few people would acquire such an encyclopaedic knowledge of the case.

Police records show that they were still pursuing a man known as 'Leather Apron' and that a net appeared to be tightening around him. Police in Holloway's Y Division recorded that two doctors had submitted reports at the local station about their suspicions of a lunatic butcher named Joseph Isenschmid. The police soon located the man and detained him at the station on 12 September. By the time that a sergeant from the Whitechapel police district got to Holloway Station, Isenschmid had become so mentally unstable, that he had been moved to an Infirmary in Fairfield Road. Inquiries in the area resulted in several witnesses saying that they knew Isenschmid by the name 'Leather Apron'. The police were hoping to take the Prince Albert pub landlady, Mrs Fiddymont, to the infirmary to see if she could confirm Isenschmid's identity as being the same man who entered her pub on the morning of Chapman's murder, but his doctors would not allow the identification ceremony to take place. The doctors' refusal was based upon their medical opinion that Isenschmid's participation in an identity parade might have serious negative effects on his mental health.

A report by Inspector Abberline of 18 September included the following 'Although at present we are unable to procure any evidence to connect him with the murders he appears to be the most likely person that has come under our notice,…and every effort will be made to account for his movements on the dates in question'. The decisive action taken by the Met's senior staff in reorganising the investigative unit appeared to be paying dividends. The highly respected Abberline had only recently been assigned to the case and within a few days of his arrival the police had place a likely suspect in detention.

In addition to Abberline co-ordinating the work of the detectives, the Met Commissioner, Sir Charles Warren, instructed in a memo of 15 September that all enquiries into the Whitechapel murders be focused through a single man at a higher level in the force. So on the same day that Abberline was to write that that the Met had a promising suspect, Chief Inspector Donald Sutherland Swanson was made the central point of all enquiries into the murders. Sir Charles appears to have been more than a little overconfident in his force's ability to solve the murders, as in the same memo he wrote 'I am convinced that the Whitechapel Murder case is one which can be successfully grappled with if it is systematically taken in hand. I go so far as to say that I could myself in a few days unravel the mystery provided I could spare the time & give individual attention to it'. So it would appear that on 15 September, the head of the Metropolitan Police was of the opinion that his force had all the information required to solve the murders; it being a simple case of sifting the evidence and joining the dots.

It should be noted that even the search for Leather Apron was mired in confusion. Y Division had apprehended a lunatic butcher named Isenschmid thought to be known as Leather Apron, but H Division was aware of a man on its patch known by the same name. So it was thought that a second Leather Apron might still be at large in Whitechapel.

The press starting having a field day and every single newspaper printed was sold, with the masses seeming to have an unquenchable thirst for news about the Whitechapel murders. The press were seeking a villain, a monster to focus readers' minds upon. Up until that point there had been stories about violent street gangs blackmailing prostitutes or the possibility of an evil foreigner lurking in the shadows, but what was missing was a name for their sensationalist headlines. Then the press got what they no doubt were wishing for, with the name 'Leather Apron' being leaked to them. Soon after, fantasy stories began appearing in all the newspapers, of an evil night stalker who moved silently in the shadows of the rookeries. The stories about Leather Apron had a significant impact upon the early investigation into the Whitechapel murders, with Ripperologist, Paul Begg devoting a whole chapter to them in his book 'Jack The Ripper - The Facts'. Begg says that the story about Leather Apron was reported far and wide, with a story even being printed in an American newspaper that gave a description of a man, more animal than human who frequented the dark streets of Whitechapel.

As for the man given the name Leather Apron. His real name was John Pizer and he was a Jewish immigrant, whose father, brother and sister lived with their respective families at 22 Mulberry Street, Whitechapel. Pizer did not live with his other family members and seems, like thousands of others, to have slept in common lodging houses. When Pizer heard the stories being written about him in the newspapers, he is thought to have become frightened for his life. The prostitutes of Whitechapel might recoil in terror at the sound of his name, but he knew that if he were identified walking along the street, the crowd would soon be baying for his blood. With this in mind, he hid himself away in his family home in Mulberry Street and waited for the drama to unfold around him.

Probably acting on a tip-off, H Division's Sergeant Thicke and a few police constables called round at 22 Mulberry Street and were surprised to find the front door opened to them by Pizer, who appeared pleased to see them. Thicke informed Pizer that he was seeking a man known to him as Leather Apron and arrested him on suspicion of committing the Whitechapel murders. Pizer actually disputed that he was known as Leather Apron, but was more than happy to be arrested and taken by arresting officers to the relative safety of a police station. Under questioning, Pizer provided alibis for his movements on the nights of the murders and was allowed to go free. Pizer had been able to prove beyond any doubt that he was in the district of Holloway in the London borough of Islington on the night of Polly Nichols' murder. So the fallen women of Holloway were most likely telling the truth when they reported being accosted by a man they knew as Leather Apron, as it was likely that they were referring to Pizer rather than Isenschmid when they made their statements.

H Division's Sergeant Thicke would surface again in 1902 in an unrelated matter. Thicke was born on 20 November 1845 in Salisbury, Wiltshire. He joined the Met on 6 March 1868 and was a member of Whitechapel's H Division between 1886 and 1893. Like Inspector Reid, he was involved in the whole investigation into the Whitechapel murders. He is remembered today for being Leather Apron's arresting officer. Thicke was well known to Whitechapel's law-breakers in the 1880s. They knew him as 'Johnny Upright' because he was known to be very upright in both his way of walking and in his policing methods.

In 1902 the American author, Jack London, visited London in order to perform research for his book 'The People of the Abyss'. He wanted to walk the metropolis' rookeries, to experience at first hand the poverty of London's poor, and wanted a safe haven in the East End into which he could retreat for a change of clothes. He was advised by a convicted felon to seek the assistance of a Whitechapel police officer, known as 'Johnny Upright'. The story goes that London arrived at Sergeant Thicke's house in beggar's attire and was given short shrift by the officer. In order to convince Thicke that he was no beggar,

London returned to Thicke's home in a hansom cab and wearing attire befitting his station. The sergeant is said to have invited London into to his house for tea and went on to find him a bolthole in the very same street that he and his family lived in. London was so impressed by these events that he went on to write about them in his book.

Unfortunately for the press, the stories about Leather Apron were soon to lose their appeal to the masses. The police had not leaked details of their prime suspect Joseph Isenschmid, and Pizer had been able to prove his innocence. However, having had his pseudonym plastered over half the world, Pizer was called as a witness at Chapman's inquest to make it clear to the jury, members of the public in the visitor's gallery and especially the journalists of the newspapers, that he was an innocent man and should be left unmolested to get on with the rest of his life.

The inquest into Annie Chapman's murder made for a grisly soap opera with the gory details of her injuries being reported in the daily newspapers. Five sessions were held in total, running from 10 to 26 September. An eyewitness, Mrs Elizabeth Long, testified to seeing a man with woman close to 29 Hanbury Street at 5.30am, very close to Chapman's estimated time of death. Mrs Long stated that the man she saw 'was of shabby-genteel appearance, was dark, wore a brown low-crown felt hat, a dark coat and had the look of a foreigner'. So at the end of the month, the usual verdict of 'wilful murder against a person or persons unknown' was made by the jury, leaving the press without any more attention grabbing headlines.

The masses, having worked themselves into a frenzy, were beginning to lose faith in the authorities. The newspapers, especially The Star, had been highly critical of Sir Charles Warren even before the Whitechapel murders and now started to go to town on him. However, criticism did not stop at the Commissioner of the Metropolitan

Police, no, now the newspapers started to focus their attention on Warren's boss, the then Home Secretary, Sir Henry Matthews. The Star wrote stories about Matthews which included descriptions of his being 'a feeble, forcible red-tapeist, with the mind of a dancing master and the statesmanship of an attorney's clerk'. Local people started to take matters into their own hands, with local tradesmen holding meetings in pubs and the working men's clubs. Mid way through September one of these groups took the name of 'The Whitechapel Vigilance Committee'. It consisted of 16 men and was led by a local builder, named George Lusk. The members' aims were mainly peaceful, their primary task being to petition the Home Secretary into sanctioning a reward for the capture of the murderer. However, they also took it upon themselves to carry out nightly patrols of the streets of Whitechapel, with each man taking nothing more than a stick and whistle for protection.

Wellcome did not take much notice of the efforts of the police, seeing them as a faceless body that had no impact upon his life. However, the Vigilance Committee might have struck a chord with him. He was a man literally from the Wild West of America, a man born to a frontier family. In the early 1880s, only a few years after Wellcome had moved to England, the Gunfight at the OK Corral took place and Billy the Kid and Jessie James had been shot dead. The law in Wellcome's eyes was not some officious invisible body of men in blue uniforms. No the law to Wellcome was the sheriff and his posse, and in September of 1888 a new posse had been formed and its sheriff was George Lusk.

CHAPTER SIXTEEN

The Ripper Letters

Wellcome had had a good month. He was drawing new life from the news stories and the new macabre items added to his growing collection of curios, even though work was as busy as ever, with the preparation of the new larger factory premises in Dartford.

The Ripper was a natural showman and had over the last few weeks begun to let himself be sucked-in by all the media attention into the killings. Up until now his fantasies revolved around performing surgery just like his uncle used to do, but this was no longer going to be enough for him. He was reading about his activities in the newspapers but he was anonymous, he did not have a name. The press had sold many a newspaper off the back of the Leather Apron headlines but that name meant nothing to him. He had been ripping-up woman like his uncle. Why not give himself a trade name? What about 'Jacob the Ripper'? No, that didn't have the right ring to it. What about 'Jack the Ripper'? Yes, that would do just fine.

The Ripper remembered letters he had sent in his youth, his little tricks and jokes. Now he would play more of his funny little games. He decided that he would write a little letter of introduction to the press. He knew how the press worked from his involvement in the production of advertisements for his company's products. He would not waste time on writing to a single newspaper. No, he would send his letter to all of them in one hit, by addressing it to the Central News Agency.

On 17 September, the Ripper wrote the first of his letters with his new pen name. He wrote in his worst handwriting, so as to disguise his own hand and what he wrote was barely legible. The press and the police had by this time received hundreds of letters relating to the murders, so no one at the Central News Agency was to take his letter seriously.

His letter read:

Dear Boss

So now they say I am a Yid when will they learn Dear Old Boss? You an me know the truth don't we. Lusk can look forever hell never find me but I am rite under his nose all the time. I watch them looking for me and it gives me the fits ha ha I love my work an I shant stop until I get buckled and even then watch out for your old pal Jacky.

Catch me if you Can
Jack the Ripper

Sorry about the blood still messy from the last one. What a pretty necklace I gave her.

There are certain words used in this letter that make it sound like the work of an American. The words: boss, buckled and pal all being Americanisms.

The word buckled grabs an Englishman's attention, but for the wrong reason. To a 19th century Englishman the word might refer to the author of the letter getting caught by the police. However in 19th century American slang, buckled also meant to get married. So it is a possibility that the Ripper was speaking from the heart when he wrote this letter. In that he felt that the only thing that might halt his killing spree would be his getting married, and even he was not sure that doing so would cure him of his blood lust.

There is also a line in the letter that appears to allude to the throwing of Chapman's intestines over her right shoulder. This is the view taken by Ripperologist John J. Eddleston in his book 'Jack the Ripper - An Encyclopaedia'. Eddleston wrote that at the 14 September inquest, Dr George Bagster Phillips provided details of two horrendous wounds made to Annie Chapman's neck but made no mention of the mutilations to her abdomen. So it is quite possible that the author of the letter was referring to something other than the wounds to Annie's neck when he wrote about giving her a pretty necklace. That something (her intestines being placed over her neck) only being known to the doctors, the police and the Ripper. My final comment on the letter is that it makes direct reference to Lusk. There is definitely something about Lusk and his Vigilance Committee that caught the Ripper's attention. It being possible that the Ripper saw Lusk and the Vigilance Committee as a force against whom he must do battle.

The Ripper was to be disappointed after the sending of this first letter. He had given the press the perfect name for their monster 'Jack the Ripper', but they did not use it. He had deliberately written the letter in highly disguised hand writing to make it look the work of a commoner. He now reasoned that someone at the Central Press Agency had not been able to decipher his scrawl and had likely consigned his letter to the waste bin. He decided to try again. His second letter was written in a more educated hand, the writing being much closer to his own. He decided to take a chance on being detected, as he wanted to ensure that someone with authority at the CPA would actually read it and act upon it. The second letter was dated 25 September, but was not posted until Thursday 27 September. The Ripper was planning to make an impact. He had planned another murder, but this time he would leave more than a body at the scene of the crime.

The second letter read:

Dear Boss,

I keep on hearing the police have caught me but they won't fix me just yet. I have laughed when they look so clever and talk about being on the right track. The joke about Leather Apron gave me real fits. I am down on whores and I shan't quit ripping them till I don get buckled. Grand work the last job was. I gave the lady no time to squeal. How can they catch me now. I love my work and want to start again. You will soon hear of me with my funny little games. I saved some of the proper red stuff in a ginger beer bottle over the last job to write with but it went thick like glue and I can't use it. Red ink is fit enough I hope ha ha. The next job I shall clip the ladys ears off and send to the police officers just for jolly wouldn't you. Keep this letter back till I do a bit more work, then give it out straight. My knife's so nice and sharp I want to get to work right away if I get the chance.

Good luck,
Yours truly
Jack the Ripper
Don't mind me giving the trade name
Wasn't good enough to post this before I got all the red ink off my hands curse it. No luck yet. They say I'm a doctor now ha ha.

A long time had now passed since Chapman's death and the Ripper was ready to kill again.

Wellcome was a very clever man. He could not have failed to notice that the police and the press appeared to have made up their minds that a foreigner - a Jew - was responsible for the murders. It was a shame that they had let old Leather Apron go. But what Wellcome did not know was that the police had a second Leather Apron in detection. This man was an insane butcher, a man who was too mentally unstable to interviewed, a man that fitted the description provided by Mrs Fiddymont, a man whose name was known to Sir Charles Warren, Commissioner of the Metropolitan Police. If the Ripper had not killed again, it is safe to assume that the police thought they had their man and Joseph Isenschmid would have felt the full force of the law.

Even if the Ripper had known all this, it might not have made any difference to him. He was again in a deep depression and needed to plan his funny little games. They were the only things keeping him 'sane'. In an insane world, planning sadistic murders was the only activity that allowed him some peace of mind.

CHAPTER SEVENTEEN

The Double Event

Early in the morning of Sunday 30 September two women's lives would end, but for evermore they would be linked together in the fabric of Ripper folklore.

Elizabeth Stride (nee Ericson), aka Long Liz was born on 27 November 1843 and was soon be 45 years of age. She was about 5 feet 2 inches in height, with dark brown curly hair, grey eyes and was missing her upper front teeth. She was the second of four children born on a small farm in the parish of Hisingen, north of Gothenburg on the west coast of Sweden. Sometime in February 1861 Elizabeth secured a job as a maid in the parish of Majorna in Gothenburg. She stayed in the job until February of 1864, when her life started to fall apart. Elizabeth's mother died in August 1864 and a month later she discovered that she was pregnant.

Things were only going to go from bad to worse for Elizabeth. On 4 April 1865 she visited hospital and was diagnosed with condyloma - genital warts, and this was followed by her giving birth to a stillborn girl on 21 April. Four months later Liz returned to hospital and was diagnosed and treated for Chancre - a highly contagious ulcer that forms in the primary stage of syphilis. In October Liz was to show-up in the Swedish police records, her discharge sheet of November that year recording her profession as being a prostitute. However, against the odds, she managed to secure a job prior to her release from custody, working as maid in the employment of a woman named Maria Wejsner. However, Wejsner appears to have employed a large number of maids, the inference being that she was a brothel keeper.

In 1866 Liz's bitter sweet existence took a turn for the better when she inherited 65 Swedish Kroner from her mother's estate. This was a fair sum of money back then and she used it to start life anew in another country, hopefully leaving behind her life as a prostitute forever. She left Sweden for London on 7 February 1866 and three years later on 7 March 1869, Liz married a man named John Thomas Stride, a carpenter by trade, and the couple went on to open a coffee shop on Upper North Street in the London borough of Poplar. So by 1869 Liz seemed to have turned her life around, having used her inheritance to transform herself from a young Swedish prostitute into a respectable married woman. However, life in Victorian Britain was precarious, it took little to send the lives of those living at the lower end of society, from relative stability into chaos and spirals of despair. In a world reliant on private charity rather than state welfare, a few minor mishaps were all that were required to steer a woman's life into a state of permanent decline.

On 21 March 1877 Liz appeared before the Thames Magistrates' Court in London before being taken to the Poplar Workhouse. Records of the Swedish Church in London show that in January 1879 she sought financial assistance from them, stating that her husband was suffering from an illness. It is not known if John Stride was ill in 1877, but in August 1884 he was admitted to the Poplar Workhouse and transferred from there to the Poplar & Stepney Sick Asylum, where he died on 24 October. The couple's marriage had ended in 1881, most likely as a result of Liz's heavy drinking and by 1884 she had returned to a life of prostitution. On 13 November 1884 records show that Liz was sentenced to seven day's hard labour for being drunk, disorderly and soliciting. Liz tried to find regular work when she could and would sometimes perform cleaning jobs for the local Jewish families. It is believed that Liz had a talent for languages and may well have taught herself Yiddish, being thought able to converse with members of the Jewish community in their own language.

In 1885 Liz met a man named Michael Kidney and she lived with Kidney for the rest of what remained of her life. During their three years together Liz would leave Kidney for weeks at a time, in all the couple were apart for about a total of five months. Kidney would state at Liz's inquest that their separations were the result of her drinking. Their relationship is likely to have been a violent one. On 6 April 1887, Liz accused Kidney of assaulting her but did not turn up at the court to complete the prosecution against him. Liz herself was no angel and was to appear before the Magistrates on several occasions between 1887 and 1888. Her last appearance was on 16 July for the charge of being drunk and disorderly. On Tuesday 25 September, the day that the Ripper penned his second letter, Liz Stride decided again to separate from Kidney. This time there would be no reconciliation, as a few days later she would be dead.

In a strange twist of fate, a good friend of Wellcome's, the now famous Dr Barnardo, visited Liz Stride's common lodging house at 32 Flower and Dean Street on Wednesday 26 September. Dr Barnardo visited a large number of dosshouses that night and spoke to many residents about his plans to open two lodging houses specifically for children. He was to inform them that he was greatly concerned about how children were being exposed to the illicit ways of adult lodging house inhabitants, leading to their being involved in child prostitution. Dr Barnardo would later state that he remembered seeing Stride being in the kitchen of the Flower and Dean Street dosshouse. Ever the publicist he wrote a letter to The Times newspaper, published 6 October 1888, that included the following extract 'One poor creature, who had evidently been drinking, exclaimed somewhat bitterly to the following effect: "We're all up to no good, and no one cares what becomes of us. Perhaps some of us will be killed next!"...I have since visited the mortuary in which were lying the remains of the poor woman Stride, and I at once recognised her as one of those who stood around me in the kitchen'. Dr Barnardo was 43 years old at the time of the time of the Whitechapel murders and had already spent years of his life roaming the rookeries in his search for destitute children. The fact that this man, well known and trusted by the local prostitutes, trained in surgery and who knew the streets and courts where the murders took place like the back of his hand, was not lost on the police. One of Dr Barnardo's biographers, Gillian Wagner, confirmed in her book 'Barnardo' that Dr Barnardo's name was included in the police's long list of suspects. However, as we know, Dr Barnardo was not the man the police were looking for.

On the afternoon of Saturday 29 September, Liz Stride was paid 6d for cleaning the rooms at her regular lodging house at 32 Flower and Dean Street. She was seen later in the day in the Queen's Head pub on Commercial Street. Liz returned to the lodging house between 7pm and 8pm and got herself ready for another night's work, entrusting her green velvet wrap with another lodger, Catherine Lane, to look after for her. By all accounts Liz was in a cheerful mood as she headed off out into the night.

ə ə ə

The second unfortunate whose life was to end at the end of a razor sharp knife that night, was Catherine Eddowes.

Catherine Conway (nee Eddowes), was born on 14 April 1842 at Graisley Green, Wolverhampton. She was one of twelve children born to George and Catherine Eddowes. The family moved to London, living in the district of Bermondsey. Catherine's mother died when she was 13 years old, and was followed by her father when she was still only 15. Two of her sisters were by this time already working in London as domestic servants, but the youngest of the children were admitted to the Bermondsey workhouse as orphans. Catherine went back to Wolverhampton where relatives helped her to obtain work as a tin plate stamper but she soon left this job and went to live with an uncle in Birmingham. Catherine went on to find work as a tray polisher but did not stay long in that job either and spent her time moving to and from Wolverhampton.

Whilst in Birmingham she met a man who called himself Thomas Conway, but whose real name may have been Thomas Quinn. He was an ex-soldier and although relatively young when they met - being in his mid twenties - he was drawing invalidity pension from the 1st Battalion, 18th Royal Irish Regiment. Conway had been pensioned out of the army after developing heart disease whilst on tour in Bombay and Madras. Catherine and Thomas started living together in Birmingham where they had a baby girl, Catherine Ann Conway, aka Annie. The family then moved to the district of Westminster in London where they had a second child, a boy they named Thomas. The couple were to have a second son in 1873 and named him Alfred. By then Catherine had turned to drink and was in the habit of leaving her family and going off for weeks - if not months - at a time, leaving her husband to cope with bringing up a young family. Thomas was a teetotaller, so would have been more affected than most by his wife's drinking. In 1880 the couple finally parted; Catherine leaving Thomas and the children who were then living in Lower George Street, Chelsea. By 1881, as a result of the ill effects of drink, Catherine found herself living in common lodging houses in the wicked quarter mile. She to tried to make a living by working for Jewish families in Whitechapel, but turned to prostitution to make ends meet.

Catherine met a man named John Kelly whilst staying at a lodging house named Cooney's, in Flower and Dean

Street. They lived as a couple as best as their financial circumstances would allow them and treated Cooney's as the closest thing that they could call home. John was a market labourer and although he did not have a permanent job, he was able to make a living from working odd jobs in the local Spitalfields market. Their annual 'holiday', as was the case for many of east London's poor, consisted of picking hops in Kent. Even though it was not a holiday in the true sense of the words, hop picking allowed London's poor to have a break from the pollution of the city. They had to work hard, but in return they enjoyed a change of scene, fresh air and some money for their trouble. However, 1888 would prove to be a bad year for the couple. They sought work in a village named Hunton which was situated close to Maidstone in Kent, but the harvest was poor and work was sparse. So the couple decided to return back home sooner than they had planned to and were back in London on the afternoon of Friday 28 September.

Their first priority was to get enough money for a bed for the night and Kelly managed to earn them 6d, but this was not enough for them to spend the night together at Cooney's. They decided that John - as the main bread winner - should take the bed in the dosshouse as this would allow him a better night's rest than that afforded by the Shoe Lane Casual Ward. The 'luxury' of sharing a room with about ten other people in the dosshouse, supposedly offered up better possibilities of sleep than those on offer at the casual ward.

Saturday 29 September found Catherine and John penniless. Things were so bad that John pawned his boots for 2 shillings and 6 pence. This was enough money for just over three night's stay for the couple at Cooney's, but on top of this they would need to find the money for food. As to how John planned on being able to find work at the market without his boots is anyone's guess. However, the couple having a little money in their pockets, bought themselves some food and shared a breakfast together in the lodging house kitchen between 10am and 11am. They were not to know it, but it was the last time that they would ever spend time together. We do not know what the couple did during the rest of the day, but at 8.30pm Catherine was found on her own, drunk and in a crumpled heap on the Aldgate High Street in the jurisdiction of the City of London Police. The City Police were less tolerant of drunks than those within the wicked quarter mile and before long Catherine found herself being hauled-off to the Bishopsgate police station to sober-up.

※ ※ ※

Over the last few days the Ripper had been busy planning his next attack. He had taken risks before, but he thought that he would need the luck of the Devil to get through the night undetected. The police, press and the mob were seeking a Jew, and he intended to provide them with something to fuel their fear and anger.

The Ripper set off to work at about 10.30pm. It was a typical late September London night; cold and wet, but perfect for what he had in mind. He had already selected his victim. He knew the where and the how, now he just had to snare the victim. He turned from the Commercial Road into Berner Street, walking slowly until he reached the Board School. On the other side of the road, at number 40, was the International Working Men's Educational Association. The club was open to working men of all nationalities, but was in actuality frequented almost exclusively by Polish and Russian Jews. The lights were on and he could hear people singing and dancing. The local Jewish community had held another of their meetings that night and if he had timed it right the meeting should have ended and most of the more serious minded attendees should have already departed for home. The Ripper returned to the street a few minutes later, this time walking on the opposite side of the street. Between numbers 40 and 42 was Dutfield's Yard; at the top of the yard was a workshop belonging to a sack manufacturer and a disused stable. Members of the IWEA used the yard as a side entrance to the club, but tended not to interfere when the local whores took their punters into the yard for a bit of business. The Ripper quietly opened the gates and walked into the dark passage and waited. He stood in the shadows and planned to say that he was sheltering from the rain, if he was discovered.

The IWEA had been packed to the rafters. About 100 people had been there for a discussion entitled 'Why Jews Should Be Socialists'. That night's chair was a young man named Morris Eagle. The discussion ended at about 11.30pm with most of the attendees leaving the club by the street door between 11.30pm and 12.00am. By the time that the Ripper arrived there were about 20 to 30 people left in the building. They were in little groups talking, singing and dancing. Morris Eagle had left the club at 11.30pm to escort his girlfriend home and returned back there about 15 minutes later. He left the club again a little later and returned again at about 12.40am, this time he entered the club through an entrance in the yard. Despite dashing in and out of the building, he did not see Liz Stride or the Ripper in the shadows when he re-entered the building to join in some singing with his friends.

At 12.30am the rain had stopped and Liz Stride was in Berner Street with a punter. PC William Smith, 452H, passed the couple as he walked his beat heading for Commercial Street. Stride led the man into the yard, she had used it many times before and felt safe there. There was always someone around, but people knew to mind their own business and keep well away when she was busy with a punter. When the man had finished his business they both returned back onto the street. The man bade Liz goodnight and went on his way, leaving her Liz to make try and make herself look presentable for her next customer. She was in good spirits, having earned herself the 6d for cleaning at the dosshouse. She had spent that money on some food, gin and beer and now only needed some money for her night's doss and a little extra for a bit of breakfast. Business was looking-up, despite the rain and she pulled out a packet of cachous - aromatic sweetmeats - to freshen her breath.

Just then something unexpected happened. Two men entered Berner Street from Commercial Street and started walking up the road towards where Liz was standing outside the Working Men's club. The first man staggered as he walked, as if intoxicated, the second man was Israel Schwartz, a Hungarian Jew. Schwartz walked slowly behind the first man who suddenly without any warning, stopped and grabbed Liz, throwing her to the ground. Schwartz was not the bravest of men and did not want to get involved in what he thought might be a domestic dispute. He quickly ran across the road, only to be confronted by another taller man who had just stepped out of a pub. The tall man stopped in front of him and lit a clay pipe. The first man shouted 'Lipski' across the road, which Schwartz, even with his poor understanding of English, knew to be a term of racial abuse used against Jews. Schwartz was scared and started to walk quickly up the road, he sensed that the second man was following him and he broke into a run and did not stop running until the tall man was nowhere to be seen.

Unbeknown to Schwartz, the first man did not know Liz Stride, he was just another of the wicked quarter mile's drunken criminals. The man had recognised Liz as a prostitute and meant to rob her. He pushed her to the ground and shouted across the road at the Jew, warning him to mind his own business. A second man had appeared, but he knew what was good for him and followed the Jewish looking man up the road, leaving Liz's attacker to get on with his assault in peace.

Liz's attacker roughed her up a little, but did not want to hurt her, he just wanted to scare her into handing over what money she had. Liz gave him her money and watched as he staggered his way along to the end of the road. He had gotten enough money from her to cover his doss and was now keen to get his head down at a lodging house before it started raining again. As for the whore, she would just have to take her chances.

Liz was not hurt, but she was a little shaken and upset. It was then that the Ripper made his move. He left the shadows, in the back of the yard, appearing as out of nowhere on the pavement beside her. He gave Liz a bit of a start but then asked her if she needed any help. Liz noticed that the man was quite well dressed and thought that he must belong to the club. Then suddenly, without warning, the man pulled her into the yard. Liz tried to fend him off but he pushed her to the ground and in one quick movement it was over. The Ripper was now becoming something of an expert in the art of murder and with one stroke of his razor sharp surgeon's knife he had cut simultaneously through the whore's windpipe and carotid artery. She would not give him any trouble now, as he listened in the darkness as she tried to breathe through her severed windpipe, the blood gushing from the gaping wound in her neck to the rhythm of her weakening heartbeat. The Ripper had great plans for this little whore, but knew that he had very little time available to him. He was just about to make his trade mark second incision into her neck when he heard the sound of a pony and trap in the road. He almost could not believe what was happening; first the whore was robbed before his eyes, now a vehicle looked like it was turning into the yard. He knew that there was a stable at the back of the yard, but it had looked like it hadn't been used for months, he could not believe that someone had chosen that night and that moment to make use of it. The Ripper let go of his victim and moved into the dark at the back of the yard. He was watching when the pony, spooked by the dying woman, veered to its left and stopped. The driver of the trap could sense that something was wrong but it was difficult for him to see in the darkness of the yard.

Louis Diemshutz was a 26-year-old Russian Jew and he and his wife were Stewards of the club. To help make ends meet Louis spent Saturdays hawking cheap jewellery at the Westow Hill market in Crystal Palace. Trade had been bad that day on account of the bad weather, so he had returned home earlier than usual. Normally he would have taken his pony straight to the stables in George Yard. However, having more unsold wares than usual, he'd decided to leave his unsold stock with his wife at the club before making his way to the stables. For all the Ripper's meticulous planning, he could not have envisaged anyone driving a trap into the yard.

Diemschutz had seen what he thought to be a pile of rags on the floor next to the wall on the right hand side of the yard. He prodded at it with his horsewhip. It was windy, but he tried to light a match to throw some light on the scene. The match quickly blew out, but not before he was able to see the woman lying in a pool of blood. His first thought was for his wife, so he ran through the club's main entrance, hoping that he would find her safe and sound within the building.

The Ripper had by now worked himself into frenzy and wanted to get to work on the whore. He had made grand plans but they all seemed lost to him now. He watched the man run into the club and knew that very soon the yard would be full of people. He wanted to finish the whore off, but regained some composure, took a deep breath and walked up the yard, past the body of Stride and turned into Berner Street. A few seconds later he took a right turn into

Fairclough Street, and he was gone, heading back to the City of London.

Louis Diemschutz had mixed emotions. He had found his wife almost immediately on entering the building. She had been in the ground floor kitchen with some of the guests and so was safe and sound. However, out in the yard lay a poor unfortunate soul, who she was he did not know, but he thought that she was dead. Diemschutz returned to the yard with another man, Isaac Kozebrodski, and lit a candle. The men, seeing the blood, decided not to touch the body and instead set off in search of a policeman.

The Ripper was also suffering mixed emotions. He'd had a grand plan and now it had gone to pot. He had killed a whore, but he had not seen the fear in her eyes or even gotten to make any meaningful cuts into her body. He hadn't even had sufficient time to make his now trademark second incision to her throat. He wondered if Mister Lusk and the police would even know if it was him that had committed the murder. He had taken a lot of chances in killing the whore at the Jews' club, but he had wanted to do more than that. He had brought some chalk with him and had planned to write a cryptic message above her body on the yard wall. This was all now going to have to wait until another day.

At first the Ripper stuck to the backstreets. He did not have much blood on him but wanted to clean himself up before venturing out onto the main roads. He found a standpipe, washed the blood from his hands and started to make his way back to the City of London and safety of Cock Lane. He was now back on the main thoroughfare, and as he walked he passed a few prostitutes and slowly the madness returned and overwhelmed him. He had walked from Whitechapel and was now in the City of London. He decided to leave the main road and ventured back into the backstreets and started to look for a suitable location in which to make a kill.

At about the same time that the Ripper had been slashing Liz Stride's throat, PC Hutt of the Bishopsgate police station was checking the cells to see if any of that night's collection of drunks was sober enough to be returned to the streets. Hutt decided that Eddowes looked sober and brought her before his sergeant to have her details recorded before letting her go on her way. Sergeant Byfield entered Catherine's details into the station log before her release, and as was usual in such cases, Eddowes gave the sergeant a false name and address for his trouble; saying that she was Mary Ann Kelly of 6 Fashion Street. PC Hutt and Catherine exchanged words as he told her the error of her ways. She was keen to know the time and PC Hutt told her that it had just gone 1.00am, it being too late for her to get herself anymore to drink that night. PC Hutt watched her leave through the station door as she turned left into the night. Whether by habit or design, Catherine had made a fateful choice. Flower and Dean Street and her temporary home lay to her right, but by choosing to go left, Eddowes headed off towards Houndsditch and the Aldgate High Street. Within 45 minutes she would be dead.

The Ripper had crossed the border from the Met's H Division into the area policed by the City Police. Although only a few minutes' walk from the rookeries of Whitechapel he could sense the different atmosphere. The streets seemed wider and cleaner and the inhabitants seemed less threatening. However, he was on uncertain ground, he did not know where he could hide or the routes taken by the City's beat officers. However, his blood was high, he had killed but had not gotten any satisfaction from it. He wanted to perform some surgery, to take a trophy or two and maybe even leave a cryptic message. Eventually he wandered into a road named Mitre Street and on turning right found himself in Mitre Square. The square was badly lit and deserted. He walked slowly around the perimeter and noticed two other access points, they were both narrow foot passages. There was a single street lamp in the square and behind it he saw the sign for a Kearley & Tonge warehouse, lights were on in the building and the door was slightly ajar. There was something familiar about that name, then he remembered it, he had worked on a whore outside another Kearley & Tonge warehouse in Buck's Row at the end of August. He was not a great believer in fate but the sight of the warehouse made him think that some hidden force had guided him to this spot so that he could complete his night's work.

Catherine Eddowes also found herself in unfamiliar territory. She was outside the wicked quarter mile and did not know the best places to display her wares, but she had no money and needed to bag herself a punter before returning to the dosshouse. Suddenly a gentleman appeared out of the shadows. He gave her a bit of a start, but then he gave her a friendly smile and bade her a good evening. He sounded like an American and did not look like a foreigner. The working girls were by now a little wary of the Jews, but this punter seemed harmless enough. So she was not afraid when he led her down the poorly lit passageway into poorly lit square. There was a street lamp on the right hand side, but the Ripper guided his intended victim away from there into a corner at the other end of the square, furthest from the light and shielded from the main street. Catherine could not see much but the Ripper could just make out the glint in her eyes as they reflected the light of the distant lamp. Then he was on her in a flash. He grabbed her around the throat, forcing her to the ground. Catherine tried to scream, but Ripper's grip was tight and just like the others she could not breathe. She passed out and was soon to pass away. The Ripper was keen to get to work and dispatched the whore with his trademark two incisions into her neck, he was sure that there would be no mistaking this whore as one of his victims. He lifted her skirts and ripped into her body. He placed the whore's intestines over her right shoulder as required by the rituals of the Brotherhood and set to work on collecting his trophies. He had difficulty seeing in the low light generated by the distant street lamp but then he found what he was looking for. He carefully sliced through some body fat and cut the kidney from the body. He collected the body parts that he had removed from the whore's body and folded them up in a cloth. Then he remembered that he had written that he would clip off an ear. He was not sure what was driving him now, but instead of the taking an ear, he set about her face, cutting into her eyelids. He cut two V's into her checks, one of each side of her face and fancied that they looked like a W. He had planned to leave a chalked message on the wall over the body of the whore in the yard next to the Jewish club and now he wanted to leave a message next to the body of this whore, but he was out of the Jewish quarter now and didn't think that his message would convey the same meaning so far away from the Jewish community. The clock was ticking and he was keen get out of the square. Quickly he cut away a piece of the whore's apron and put it in his pocket. He still had not taken an ear and was just about to cut one away when he heard the unmistakable sound of a beat officer's boots coming from the direction of Mitre Street. The Ripper sliced into the whore's ear, but left it dangling. Instinct made him move to the far end of the yard, away from the policeman's approaching footsteps. He entered the narrow passageway and was away into the night.

The time now was 1.45am and about three quarters of an hour had passed since the discovery of Liz Stride's body by the officers of the Metropolitan Police. PC Edward Watkins of the City Police entered Mitre Square from Mitre Street, he had inspected it only fifteen minutes earlier, it was deserted then and appeared to be the same now. All was clear from where he was standing down to the street lamp at the far end of the square. He turned to his right as he had done earlier that night and directed the light of his belt lantern into the dark corners of the square. Then a sight met his eyes that he had not seen in all his 17 years as a policeman; directly in front of him he saw the body of a woman that he would later describe as being 'ripped up like a pig in the market'. Watkins' first reaction was to run to the light coming from the warehouse at the end of the square. He burst through the open door and shouted for assistance. The warehouseman, George Morris, was an ex Met policeman and together the two men returned to the body in the square. It was obvious to them that there was nothing that could be done as the woman was clearly dead, so they ran into the streets around Mitre Square shouting for the assistance of more policemen. The City Police descended upon the square and at once set about searching the local streets for the murderer.

The Ripper had taken many risks in the performance of his crimes, but his actions on the night of the double event defy explanation. He had taken a huge risk in killing a woman in the yard next to the Jewish club, he had taken a much greater risk in his unplanned murder of the second woman in Mitre square and now he was to take another. Instead of trying to escape from the area, heading further west into the City of London and towards the safety of Cock Lane, he doubled-back returning to Whitechapel. There were now police officers from two police forces searching the streets on either side of him; the City Police to the West and the Met Police to the East. Officers from both forces were working their way through the backstreets, shining their lanterns into the darkness and stopping, questioning and searching all suspicious looking men in their path. And yet, the Ripper ignored all this as he had something that he wanted to do. He found himself in Goulston Street, a road in the heart of the Jewish Community of Whitechapel. He hid in the ground floor of the stairwell leading to 108-119 Wentworth Model

Dwellings. It was now that he took the chalk from his pocket and wrote his cryptic message on the wall:

The Juwes are
The men That
    Will not
Be Blamed
    For nothing

Next he took the piece of bloodstained cloth that he had cut from the whore's skirts and placed it on the floor under the newly scrawled graffiti. The blood on the cloth was wet and glistened in the half-light. He felt sure that it would attract the attention of any passing policeman. The Ripper then headed north and took a long route back to the safety of Cock Lane.

※ ※ ※

At 2.55am a policeman was retracing his steps through Goulston Street. PC Alfred Long, number 254A, was on temporary duty from Westminster's A Division (Scotland Yard) and had been drafted into Whitechapel along with many other officers to help hunt for the Ripper. PC Long was new to his beat and not yet aware of either the night's two murders. As he walked he noticed something glistening in front of him in the darkness. What he saw made his heart race. On the floor just outside a stairwell was a piece of blood-stained apron. His immediate thought was that he might have stumbled upon another Ripper murder, as he was reminded of George Yard Buildings, the scene of Martha Tabram's murder. He entered the stairwell and ran up the stairs to the top floor and was actually surprised and relieved not to have found a body. It was when he returned to the ground floor, that he noticed the writing on the wall, written in white chalk on the fascia of the black bricks.. The writing looked fresh and he felt sure was connected to the blood-stained piece of cloth. Thinking that it might be a clue, PC Long arranged for colleague to guard the writing and stop anyone from entering or leaving the building. He then sped off to the Commercial Street police station with the piece of blood stained apron in his hand.

At 3.05am, a concerned Superintendent Arnold of the Met Police found himself in Goulston Street, reading some writing chalked on a wall at the bottom of a tenement stairwell. It was clear to him that his junior police officers thought that the Whitechapel Murderer had written the message and that thought the killer to be a member of the Jewish community. If his officers thought this, then the mob were going to think the same and their reaction to the message was likely to be very much less controlled. The streets were relatively empty but within a few hours the street market would be in full swing and then many hundreds of people would have the opportunity of seeing the writing. Arnold's gut feeling was that the message might cause an anti-Jewish riot and felt that it should be washed away before the morning market crowds had a chance to see it. An inspector was left in charge with a wet sponge and instructed to keep members of the public away from the stairwell until further notice.

At 3.45am a Superintendent McWilliam arrived at the stairwell and on seeing the writing immediately ordered that a photographer be found to photograph it for the record. What happened next was to fuel conspiracy theories up until the present day.

Up until the double event, Sir Charles Warren, the head of the Metropolitan Police had infrequently ventured into Whitechapel to view any of the murder scenes. However, that particular morning, he had dragged himself out of bed and was at the Lehman Street police station at 5.00am.

Then before visiting either of the murder scenes he went to Goulston Street to read the writing at the foot of the stairwell with his own eyes. Sir Charles agreed with the view of Superintendent Arnold that the writing should be washed away before any of the street vendors or market shoppers got the chance to see it. There appears to have been no time to photograph the message in the early morning darkness. So Sir Charles instructed that the message be copied exactly as seen, matching as closely as possible the style of writing of the hand that wrote it. The message was then washed from the wall, but the controversy surrounding its destruction ensured that it would never be forgotten.

※ ※ ※

To my mind the conspiracy theorists seem to have a valid point about the actions taken by the police regarding the short chalked message. We have the head of the Metropolitan Police Force not immediately visiting either murder scene, but instead appearing to be completely focused on twelve words scrawled on the stairwell wall. Theories abound that Warren, as one of Britain's leading Freemasons, immediately recognised the word 'Juwes' as coming from a Masonic ritual. So the author of the message had used a word, whose meaning was known only to the senior Masons, those men who had advanced beyond the order's lowest three degrees. No man allowed through the Royal Arch would likely loiter in a tenement stairwell in Goulston Street unless he, just like Sir Charles Warren, had a very good reason for being there.

If such conjecture were in fact true, then the sight of the message would have struck fear into hearts of Sir Charles Warren, Assistant Commissioner Dr Robert Anderson and other members of the British Establishment. As they would now have known that they were not dealing with any ordinary madman. No, the Whitechapel 'maniac' was a man capable of committing two murders within the space of an hour, savagely mutilating one of the bodies, and then having the presence of mind to cut away a portion of the victim's bloodstained apron so that he could use it to flag an anti-Jewish 'Masonic' cryptic message written on a stairwell wall in the heart of London's Jewish community. Actions such as these should have required the skill and nerve of a secret agent, not some demented madman, and especially not a man forced to live from hand to mouth in Whitechapel's dosshouses. If Sir Charles Warren thought this to be the case, it might go some way to explaining why he had chosen that particular day to drag himself out of bed, and personally direct operations on that cold, wet Sunday morning.

I have included two maps, one for each of the two murders

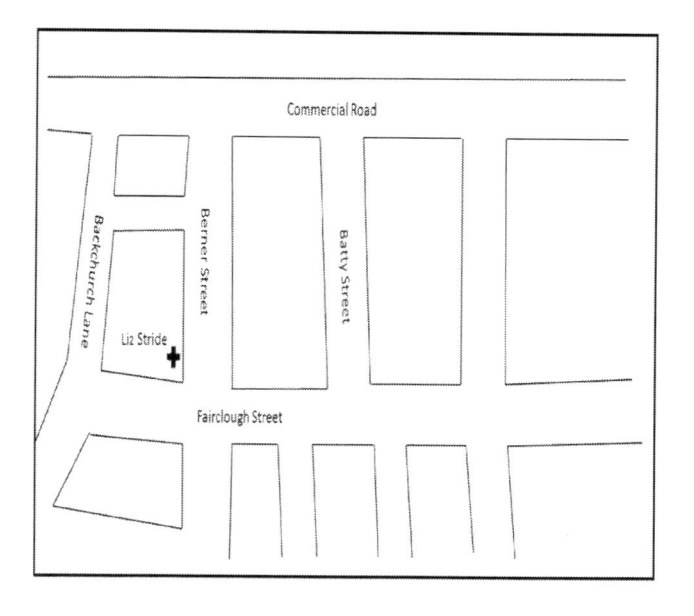

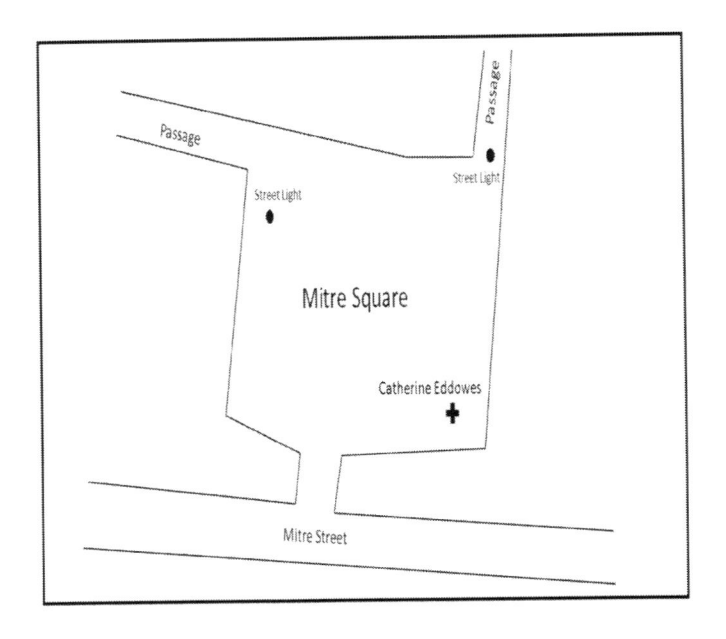

CHAPTER EIGHTEEN

A Legend is Born

All hell broke loose after the double murder. The streets of Whitechapel were again packed with thousands of frightened people baying for the blood of the killer. A memo written by a senior Home Office official recorded that Queen Victoria herself telephoned the Secretary of State asking for information about the murders. There would now have been huge pressure on the authorities to arrest someone, anyone for the heinous crimes.

In one stroke Sir Charles Warren's life had been turned upside down by the Ripper. He had wrongly assumed that the case was almost closed, with it simply being a matter of time before the mad butcher, Joseph Isenschmid, was formally and publicly announced as being responsible for the murders. Now there had been two more murders, committed whilst his prime suspect was safely tucked away in a lunatic asylum. Added to this, the real killer now appeared to be highly intelligent, cold, calculating and possibly worst of all, might possibly be a brother Freemason. This would have placed Warren in a bit of a quandary, as by the rites of the Brotherhood, he would be duty bound to protect the killer – a fellow Royal Arch Freemason - from prosecution. The case was now far from closed and Joseph Isenschmid was quietly lost to history.

The police response was immediate with over 100 additional uniformed officers drafted into Whitechapel's H Division as temporary cover. The additional blue uniforms being assigned to the streets were as much to reassure the public that something was being done as to help catch the killer. In addition to the uniformed officers, many plainclothes officers were placed on duty, some even disguised as women. In a way this actually proved to be counterproductive as there were now many new unfamiliar male faces to be seen in the wicked quarter mile, and left the police chasing their own tails.

Another action taken by the police was to meet with great public approval. Sir Charles Warren authorised the use of two specially trained bloodhounds - Barnaby and Burgho - to be kept in reserve for the investigation of any future murder scene. The hope was that the dogs would be able to track the miscreant from the crime scene back to his lair. Successful trials were conducted with the dogs in one of London's parks but some scepticism was voiced as to how well the dogs would perform in a crowed city. However, the vast majority of the press and the public, thought the commissioning of the dogs to be the first sensible act taken by the authorities since the murders had begun. Sir Charles had finally scored points with the masses for one of his decisions. However, behind the scenes, funding for the dogs had yet to be approved by the Home Office, a Government Office led by Warren's now arch enemy, Home Secretary, Sir Henry Matthews.

Lusk's Whitechapel Vigilance Committee again pushed for the offer of a Government sponsored reward, payable for information leading to the capture of the killer. They also made a new suggestion that met with Warren's immediate approval. They asked for a free pardon to be granted to any accomplice of the Ripper, proven not to have actively participated in physical act of murder of any of the fallen women. The hope was that someone closely connected to the killer would turn him in. However, this request fell on deaf ears at the Home Office. Home Secretary Matthews knew that any change in policy would make him look indecisive and weak, and so might result in him and not Warren losing his job. No, Matthews had other plans; he wanted the killer captured, but needed all the failings of the authorities to date, to be pointed clearly in the direction of his Commissioner of Police. However, October 1888 will be remembered predominantly for one thing, it is the month that a legend was born.

As promised in his letter dated 25 September to the Central News Agency, the Ripper followed it up with a postcard. His weekend's work had gone brilliantly with him capturing victory out of the jaws of defeat. The only thing that had not gone to plan was that his message in Goulston Street had been washed away before anyone had seen it.

The post card read:

I was not codding deal old Boss when I
gave you the tip, you'll hear about Saucy
Jacky's work tomorrow double event this
time number one squealed a bit couldn't
finish straight off. Had not got time to get
ears for police thanks for keeping last
letter back till I got work again.
Jack the Ripper.

He was careful to write in a similar hand to his last letter and posted the card from the same EC posting district, close to the Burroughs Wellcome offices in Snow Hill.

The CNA received the postcard on 1 October and quickly located the letter written in the same hand dated 25 September. They had treated the letter as just another hoax, but now they were not so sure. The letter and postcard were sent to Chief Constable Williamson of Scotland Yard, who had them forwarded immediately to the Central Office of the Metropolitan Police. The police took the letter and postcard very seriously, as they thought that the correspondence hinted at information that only the killer would have known. If genuine, they thought that this could be the killer's first real mistake, as they now possessed copies of his handwriting - even if heavily disguised - and had the means of making the writing known to the public at large. A poster was prepared on 3 October and included facsimile copies of the letter and postcard. The very next day the poster was placed outside every police station in London and facsimile copies were returned to the CNA with permission for them to be published in newspapers throughout the land. However, in publishing the documents, the police had given the press and the masses what they had been craving for, it gave them a name to latch onto. The 'Leather Apron' had been good whilst it had lasted but no name was quite likely to have caught the public imagination better than 'Jack the Ripper'.

The press headlines more than satisfied Wellcome's fantasies. However, there was now a strong emphasis on the killer being American in origin, the Americanisms in the letter and postcard not being lost on the police or the media. At the same time as details of the Ripper's correspondence hit the streets, a story appeared in the 4 October edition of the Evening News that would cast further suspicion on men from the North American continent. The Evening News reported that a local fruit trader, Matthew Packer, had sold a bunch of grapes to Liz Stride and an unknown mystery man shortly before her murder. Credence was added to the story as Packer was said to have correctly identified Stride's body at the mortuary. As Packer's fruit stall was only two doors down from the International Working Men's Association club, people took his story seriously indeed. Responding to leading questions asked by the newspaper's reporter, Packer described the mystery man as wearing an American style felt hat and speaking with a 'Yankee' twang.

The Ripper appears to have gone to considerable lengths to create anti-Jewish feeling in Whitechapel, so he is unlikely to have been best pleased with Packer's story or the analysis of his letters.

❦ ❦ ❦

Later in the month, the Ripper made contact with the sheriff. On 15 October he sent Lusk a note and a gift.

The note read:

Sor,
I send you half the Kidne I took from
One woman prasarved it for you tother
piece I fried and ate it was very nise I may
send you the bloody knif that took it out
if you only wate a whil longer

signed Catch me when
you can
Mishter Lusk.

Enclosed with the note was half a kidney.

Lusk at first thought that the package he had received through the post was some sort of sick hoax, but it disturbed him none the less. So he mentioned receipt of the half kidney at the following night's Vigilance Committee meeting. It being very late (12.30am) the committee decided that a few members would visit Lusk at home later in the morning to make a decision on what to do with the object. So later that morning a few committee members, led by the Treasurer, Joseph Aarons, viewed the kidney. They agreed that it was most likely the work of a hoaxer, with the kidney most likely cut from body of an animal. However, their interest piqued, they arranged for it to be inspected by a member of the medical profession. However, the response they received back from their medical expert was to alarm them. Dr Openshaw of the

London Hospital informed them that the kidney was not from an animal but was definitely human and had been removed from the left-hand-side of the body. The committee still thought it probable that the kidney had been sent to Lusk by a hoaxer, but they were now more concerned as the Whitechapel murderer had removed Catherine Eddowes' left kidney from her body. With that they decided to give the kidney over to the police for further analysis. The police doctors confirmed that it was a left-sided human kidney, adding that it came from a person with Bright's disease. Eddowes' autopsy had shown that her remaining right-sided kidney also showed signs of the same disease, greatly increasing the possibility that the Ripper had actually been responsible for Lusk's gruesome gift.

It only remains to be said that the local police must have known in October 1888 that they were well out of their depth. The likes of Sergeant Thicke, Inspectors Reid and Abberline and Chief Inspector Swanson had never dealt with such a case before. Normally when a murder was committed there was always a connection between the killer and the victim. In the case of the Whitechapel murders there appeared to be no relationship between the victims and their killer. The police on the ground were supposed to act as the Met's lightning rod, attracting information into the force through their web of informants, spread out amongst the local Whitechapel community. They certainly received a lot of information, but none of it was to their advantage. The CID and H Division must have decided, that either this man would be caught literally red-handed in the act of murder, or not at all.

CHAPTER NINETEEN

The Blame Game

By November 1888 Henry Wellcome was depressed again; the Whitechapel murderer had not killed for a whole month. The Ripper's fantasies were in full flow and he was busy planning his next act. He would have to be very smart from now on as the police were flooding the streets of Whitechapel and its wicked quarter mile with officers, both in uniform and plain clothes. Most of the fallen women had returned to their local streets to earn their doss money, but it would be much harder to entrap one now as they were very much on their guard, many having taken to carrying knives for their protection. However, as always, the Ripper had a plan, he knew how the game could be played.

Friday 9 November was the date of the Lord Mayor's show. This was to be the day on which the Right Honourable James Whitehead, the new Lord Mayor of London, would drive in his mayoral carriage through London's streets to make his oath of office at the Royal Courts of Justice in the Strand. The masses would turn out in their thousands to see all the pomp and pageantry of the paraded, and as always on these occasions, the masses would need to be managed, they would need to be policed. It is not known how many officers were removed from duty on the night of Thursday 8 November and allocated to crowd control along the route of the Lord Mayor's parade, but however many it was it was enough to allow the Ripper to get back out to work undetected.

※ ※ ※

In the midst of the all the activity related to the Ripper, a private battle was being fought. The Home Secretary, Sir Henry Matthews and the Met Police Commissioner, Sir Charles Warren had been at loggerheads for over a month, each trying to save his job and reputation by hinting at the failings of the other for the authorities' failure to apprehend the murderer. Matthews, being the more senior ranking figure, had the upper hand but Warren had been playing a straight bat and had been very careful not to accept personal blame in any of his correspondence relating to the investigation. Matthews was in trouble, he had not authorised a reward for capture of the Whitechapel murderer and as the killings mounted the criticism levelled against him started increasing at an exponential rate. Warren had been keen on Lusk's suggestion for a special pardon for accomplices to the murderer, as he was becoming convinced that one man working alone could not have carried out the murders. On 13 October Warren had even mooted the idea of a secret society being responsible for the crimes. However, Home Secretary Matthews had blocked the idea of a pardon, probably on the grounds that he had not thought of it first. The two men appeared to be unable to agree on anything. Even the two Bloodhounds had been stood down by the end of the month as Matthew's department had refused to authorise the dog owner's expenses. Finally Warren dropped the ball and Matthews made his move.

Sir Charles wrote an article in a periodical named Murray's Magazine, focusing on administration in the Metropolitan Police Force, that article having absolutely nothing to do with the Whitechapel murders. However, unbeknown to him a Home Office ruling had been made in 1879 forbidding any officer from publishing such material without first receiving authorisation to do so from the Home Secretary. So on 8 November Matthews wrote to Warren drawing his attention to the ruling and instructed him not to repeat the offence again. Warren blew a gasket; he refused to accept the Home Secretary's instruction and immediately tendered his resignation, which by all accounts, was very gratefully accepted. The press, especially The Star were overjoyed at the news, stating that justice had finally been done for Warren's handling of the Bloody Sunday demonstration back in 1887.

It will never be known whether Sir Charles Warren engineered his own resignation, using a matter with no connection to the Whitechapel murderers as an excuse to leave the Police Force. But under his leadership the Met Police had made absolutely no progress in solving the murders. Added to this, his sacred Masonic vows, made on his passing through the Freemason's Royal Arch, meant that even if he had known the killer's identify, he was honour bound not to disclose it. So it is possible that Warren took the easy way out, giving up his job and position in society, not through incompetence in post, but in response to a matter of high principle and personal honour. If he could not catch the killer, then this may have been the legacy he wanted to recorded in the annals of history.

Whether forced upon him by circumstance or out of personal design, Matthews had one final indignity for Warren. On taking up office Warren had argued with his then deputy, James Monroe, and Monroe being the junior of the two, resigned over their differences. Now, Warren having failed to catch the Ripper found himself being replaced by Monroe, who was hastily appointed as the new Commissioner of the Metropolitan Police.

The men on the ground continued to toil as best they could. The Ripperologist Philip Sugden informs in his 'The Complete History of Jack the Ripper', that Inspector Walter Dew recorded in his memoirs that the likes of Inspector Abberline took it upon themselves to patrol the streets of Whitechapel in their free time until 4 or 5 in the morning instead of going home to bed. Therefore we can see that the Whitechapel officers were not content to just use their skills of detection to try and catch the miscreant, and were not against the faint hope that a mixture of luck and personal endeavour might allow them to catch the miscreant in the act.

※ ※ ※

The arguments of the men at the top were not to the advantage of the destitute women of Whitechapel. As the leaders squabbled, a third man was planning a murder most savage. The Ripper had held himself back from visiting Whitechapel at night during the whole month of October. He assumed that the streets would be crawling with policemen, with orders to concentrate their efforts on both foreigners (men of Jewish appearance) and men who spoke with American accents. He also reasoned that patrols would be stepped-up over the final weekend of October and the first weekend of November, leaving a window of opportunity between the two. That window was the night before the Lord Mayor's show, the night of Thursday 8 November.

The Ripper planned to spend as little time as possible on the streets. Ideally he would like to work indoors but he did not imagine that many fallen women would be able to earn enough money to pay for their own rooms. What he wanted and what he needed was access to a room, close to one of the main thoroughfares. He tended to work off Commercial Street and the Whitechapel Road, so he planned to follow whores from these streets back to their lodgings, to those that had their own rooms. Most of the wretches took their punters into the alleys, yards and courts, so he knew to ignore such women. Most late night/early morning prostitution took place close to the Ten Bells public house on Commercial Street on account of its special licence, which allowed it to remain open when the other pubs closed at 12.30am. The Ripper chose to work close to the Ten Bells concentrating on the infamous streets of the wicked quarter mile: Dorset Street, Flower and Dean Street, Thrawl Street and Whites Row.

CHAPTER TWENTY

Mary Jane Kelly – A Tart Without a Heart

Mary Jane Davis (nee Kelly) was a young woman of about 25 years of age in 1888. She was about 5ft 7in. tall and had light waist length hair. We do not know her birth date or exactly where she was born. She was definitely from Limerick, Ireland but it is not clear whether she was born in Limerick town or County Limerick. She was one of eight or nine children born to John Kelly. The family moved from Ireland to Wales when John got a job as a foreman at an ironworks. When Mary Jane was about 16 years of age she married a coal miner who went by the surname of Davis or Davies but her husband died in a mine explosion a few years later. As with most women without means of support, Mary Jane moved to a city where there were more options for earning a living. She moved to Cardiff, living with a cousin who may have introduced her to prostitution. Then, at some stage she made the move to London. Being a young attractive woman in the prime of her life she did not immediately end up in one of London's slum areas. Instead she started work in a high-class West End brothel and is thought to have taken several trips to France. Her work may have been degrading, but Mary appears to have earned good money and was able to live the life of a lady.

It is possible that Mary Jane had willingly gone to France to work in a legalised brothel, where she thought she might make even more money than she was earning in the high-class brothels of London. In the 1880s young British women were being enticed over to the continent with promises of luxurious lifestyles, only to find that they were to live in virtual slavery, having been sold to brothel keepers who did not let them out of their premises. Mary Jane may have been one such young woman enticed into travelling to France by the promise of the good life, only to find herself locked-down in a continental brothel. If so, she may then have escaped back to England and would have been on the run from the brothel owner, who would not have taken kindly to losing his investment. There are many ifs in this theory, but if this was the case, it might explain why when still a young attractive woman, Mary found herself not in London's salubrious West End, but instead in its wicked quarter mile, penniless and whoring for her rent money.

Things need not have ended like this for Mary Jane. She had a long-time companion in a man named Joseph Barnett, a market porter by trade. The couple met for the first time on Good Friday, 18 April 1887. They immediately felt a bond between them and decided to live together. Their first home was in George Street and by a strange quirk of fate they may have been living at the same lodging house as the first Whitechapel murder victim, Emma Smith, who met her death back in April 1888. Anyhow, soon after Emma Smith's murder the couple found a room at the back of 26 Dorset Street, officially named 13 Miller's Court. Their rent was 4s 6d a week, or 54d a week, which seems to be quite a good rate considering that Annie Chapman was paying 8d per night for a twin bunk in a dosshouse.

As with the stories of the other Ripper victims, a change in personal circumstance could very quickly lead to severe monetary problems. Many a woman was forced into earning money by any means available to her, which usually meant prostituting herself on the unforgiving streets of the city's wicked quarter mile. Sometime during the month of September, Barnett lost his market job. Almost immediately the couple started to run-up rent arrears and by 9 November 1888 they owed their landlord, John McCarthy, 29s in unpaid rent. McCarthy, just like any other slum landlord was not known for his charity. Therefore, it is strange that he allowed Joseph and Mary Jane to get so far behind with their rent. If they had been staying at a dosshouse they would have been turned out onto the streets after missing a single night's payment. McCarthy also owned and ran a chandler's shop at 27 Dorset Street, which was situated at the entrance to Miller's Court, so he would have been able to keep a close eye on the couple. It isn't beyond the realms of possibility that he saw Mary Jane's potential to make money from whoring and might even have had designs on her becoming a full-time prostitute, working out of the dingy backroom that was 13 Miller's Court. However, all that is really known is that on 30 October the couple had a row and Joseph moved out leaving Mary Jane to find the rent money by her own means.

On the afternoon of Thursday 8 November Mary Jane went out drinking with a close friend of hers, a laundress named Maria Harvey. Maria had stayed with Mary Jane at Miller's court on the Monday and Tuesday nights of that week and had left a number of items of clothing in Mary Jane's room. When the pair parted company Mary Jane returned to Miller's Court on her own. Joseph Barnett arrived there shortly after and found her in the company of another Miller's Court resident, Lizzie Albrook. Lizzie remembered the couple being on good terms, with Barnett apologising to Mary for not being able to give her any money. So with outstanding rent owed to McCarthy, Mary Jane Kelly found herself out on that dreary, cold, wet Thursday night, touting for a bit of business.

* * *

At about 10.00pm the Ripper set off to complete his night's work. He had now acquired a taste for human flesh, after eating half of Catherine Eddowes' kidney. Tonight he would take another trophy, something bigger, more personal.

At 11.30pm Mary Jane was drunk and wandering up and down Commercial Street looking for clients. Many of the fallen women in Whitechapel were in their 30s and 40s and had seen far better days. Mary Jane was a lot younger than most of the other unfortunates, she was relatively tall and proud of her long flowing hair, which she liked to show off by not wearing a bonnet. In the company of the destitute woman of the wicked quarter mile, she would have walked like a giant amongst the pygmies. In all, she stood out.

The Ripper arrived in Commercial Street at about 11.00pm. He walked slowly along the road looking for his next victim. He was shabbily dressed and carried a can of beer in his hand. He was a Whitechapel regular now and knew how to dress, act and move so as not to attract too much attention to himself. He would have been nigh on invisible, if it hadn't been for his large thick red moustache. His hunch had proved right, there were not many officers of the law to be seen that night, as they had been given the night off to rest up in advance of their important duties, managing the crowds expected to line the route of the Lord Mayor's parade.

The Ripper had his eye on a potential target. He had seen the tall young whore before and had followed her to Dorset Street and into a little courtyard fronted by a chandler's shop. He knew that she was not the resident of a lodging house and guessed that she was using her own room in which to conduct her business. The Ripper was back in the wooing stage and very much needed to gain the whore's trust. He had taken many risks over the last few weeks and thought that this would be the most dangerous one yet. He knew that by entering Dorset Street and going back to the whore's room, in a yard with only a single entrance, he would have no means of escape if something went wrong. If she became suspicious of him and screamed he would most likely find himself in the clutches of the mob and hanging from the end of a rope.

The Ripper approached his target whom was clearly very drunk. He gave the whore his best smile and they got talking. She commented on the bad weather and suggested returning to her room if he was keen for a bit of company. The Ripper waved a few shillings in front of her to capture her attention. He said that he had not spent the night in the company of a woman for a long time and was willing to pay extra if she would let him stay the night with her. Mary Jane knew that her partner would not take kindly to her allowing strange man to share her bed for the whole night, but Joseph Barnett had been round earlier in the evening and did not have any money for her. She was penniless and was anticipating a call from McCarthy or one of his men chasing the overdue rent, so she agreed to the gentleman's offer. They walked slowly down Commercial Street and turned into Dorset Street. The Ripper held his breath as they approached the chandler's shop as he hoped to gain entry to the whore's room without detection. However, he had figured that even if he was seen, who was likely to remember him? Dorset Street had a number of common lodging houses, so his face would be one out of a thousand others who would wander into what would one day be called the 'Worst Street in London'.

It was about 11.45pm when another Miller's Court resident, Mary Ann Cox, a thirty-one year old widow who had been supporting herself through prostitution, was freezing and on her way back home. She too had been working on that cold, wet night and had decided to pop back to her room in Miller's Court to get herself some warmer clothing. She turned into Dorset Street just behind a couple. She soon recognised the tall figure of Mary Jane in the company of a shabbily dressed gentleman. She followed the couple past the chandler's shop into the poorly lit court. Mrs Cox said good night to Mary Jane who was so drunk that she was only barely able to respond back to her. Mrs Cox took another, better look at the man; she thought him to be about 5ft 5in. in height and about 36 years old. He seemed to have a blotchy complexion, but what she really remembered about him was his thick carroty moustache. His clothes were all dark in colour, he wore a dark overcoat and black felt hat. The man waved the pot of ale that he had been holding to distract Mrs Cox's attention away from his face. The Ripper was careful not to make any contact with this other whore and said nothing to her. He had distracted her attention with the can of beer, but he thought that even the stupidest of whores would remember his American accent, should he speak to her. Mary Jane entered her room and he followed her inside. The Ripper knew that it was far too early to kill her with so many people about and had to use all of his will power to stop himself from slipping into capture mode. No, he would not reveal his true purpose for a good while yet.

Mrs Cox heard the drunken Mary Jane break into song and shortly after midnight she made her way back out onto the streets. When Mrs Cox returned to Miller's Court at about 1.00am she noticed that the light in Mary Jane's room was still on and she could still hear her singing. Mrs Cox remained in her room for only a few minutes before venturing out yet again into the night. The courtyard was busy, what with residents popping in and out and McCarthy's chandler's shop still being open for business.

In addition to Mrs Cox, another Miller's Court resident arrived back home at about 1.00am. Elizabeth Prater, a laundress had been out from about 9.00pm, she was cold and wet, but stopped for a chat with McCarthy at his shop. She eventually entered her room at 27 Dorset Street at about 1.30am. She was alone and was in the habit of barricading the door to her room with a few chairs for additional security. Her room was directly above Mary Jane's. The walls and ceilings in the buildings were paper-thin and any unusual sounds would be detected immediately. The Ripper could hear someone dragging chairs across the floor in the room above. He had no idea why they were moving furniture as such a late hour, but it meant that they were awake, so he would have to let some more time pass before he set to work.

Mrs Cox finally returned to the courtyard at about 3.00am. She passed Mary Jane's room again, but this time all was quiet and the light was off. The Ripper had been patiently waiting. The whore had fallen asleep and he lay next to her fantasising about the work he was yet to perform. Then when he could wait no more, he finally entered capture mode. He knew that he would gain little satisfaction from killing the whore in the pitch dark of the room. He needed a little light so that he could capture the horror and terror in her eyes when he made his intentions known to her. In short, he had to let his victim know that he'd captured her. He got up and relit the single candle that the whore had placed on her bedside table. Mary Jane awoke from her alcohol-induced slumber and saw the American fiddling with his clothes and thought was that he might be intent on taking his money back and running off into the night, but she was not too alarmed, as there was something about the man that made her trust in him. The Ripper had already removed the surgeon's knife from his coat pocket and held it behind his back as he made his way back onto the bed. The whore had not seen it yet, but she soon would. He whispered a few words of reassurance to her and then in the blink of an eye his expression changed, the transformation from Jekyll into Hyde was almost instantaneous. Mary Jane saw the evil in his eyes but it was too late, the Ripper was on her in a flash. She managed one muffled cry of 'murder' before his hands grabbed tight around her throat. The Ripper was happy as he had seen the terror in her eyes before she faded away into unconsciousness. The noise of the Ripper's attack, although low, was enough to waken Mrs Prater from her slumber. Something had disturbed her baby kitten, which had walked across her body for reassurance. She thought she had heard a voice call out 'murder'. The voice seemed close, she listened intently for a few seconds, but the call was not repeated; so feeling safe in her barricaded room she fell back into a deep sleep.

The Ripper took his knife and cut into the right-hand side of the whore's neck, he preferred the left, but there was little room for manoeuvre in the small room. Blood spurted over the wall and with it, the life drained away from the whore's body. He surveyed the room whilst the woman lay dying beside him. He needed more light to help him fulfil his dreams, he'd ripped-up the others in the half-light but now he had the time and privacy in which to perform some proper surgery. He took some clothes and put them onto the dying embers of the room's fireplace. Once the fire took hold he had plenty of light with which to work. He got carried away and sliced-off the whore's body parts and placed them all about the room. Then he took his trophy, he wanted something more personal than a kidney, and decided upon the whore's heart. He played with her body, mutilating her face, then he decided to play a little game. He cut off the whore's nose and ears and turned her head so that it faced the door. Yes that would make a fine sight for those that would find her.

Then it was over. Hyde returned to Jekyll and even the Ripper was shocked by scene that met his eyes. The light of the fire burned bright, the room was very hot and covered in blood and body parts; he had truly transformed the little room into a living hell. As he cleaned himself up, the Ripper felt that he might have temporarily lost all his humanity, and for a short while had ceased to be a man and been replaced by a monster. It was not going to be easy for him, but at that precise moment he decided that the killing must stop. It was now close to 5 am and London would soon be stirring for the Lord Mayor's show. He heard movement in the room above and knew that it was time for him to leave. He carefully packed away his trophy and walked slowly out of the whore's room, through the yard and out into what remained of the night. Soon he was at the warehouse and safety. He changed his clothes, took the whore's heart and placed it in a jar containing preserving fluids. He decided that he might not eat it after all and intended to keep it hidden in plain sight amongst his numerous, gruesome curios.

Shortly after the Ripper had left Mary Jane's room, Elizabeth Prater removed the chairs which blocked access to her room, made her way downstairs and went off to the pub for a rum; thinking it a fine way to start a cold November day.

Given below is a map showing Miller's Court, Dorset and Thrawl streets.

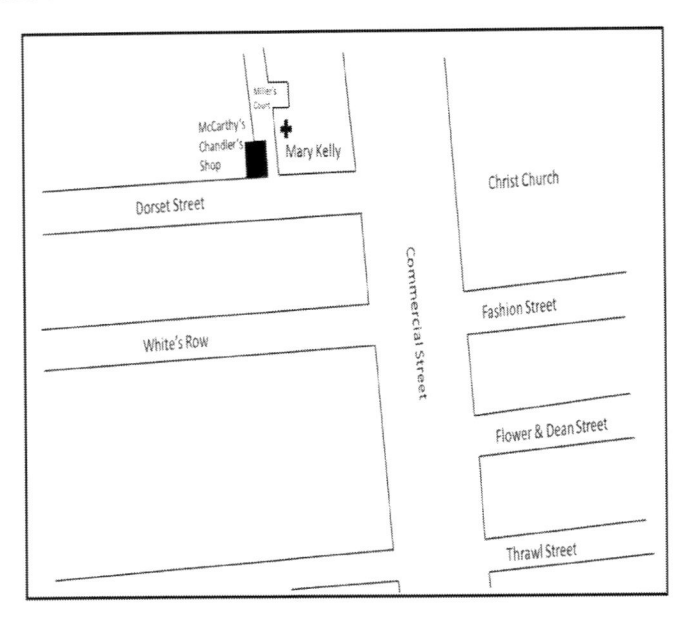

CHAPTER TWENTYONE

The End of the Carnage

At 10.45am Mary Jane's landlord, John McCarthy instructed his shop assistant, Thomas Bowyer, to knock on the door of 13 Miller's Court and try to get some long overdue rent money. McCarthy knew that Mary Jane had been out working the night before and was keen to catch her before she had the chance to spend any of her earnings on beer or rum. She and Barnett now owed him 29s and he was concerned that if the debt got any larger it was never going to be repaid. He could see that Mary Jane had the potential to make a tidy sum if she put her mind to it but he did not want her and Barnett upping sticks and moving on without paying him what he was owed.

Bowyer dutifully knocked at number 13, he knew that Mary Jane was in and did not care to wake her, but there was nothing for it, as the boss wanted his money. There was no answer from inside the room, so he peered through the broken windowpane, but did not want to believe the sight that met his eyes. When he returned to McCarthy he was barely able to speak, but tried his best to tell his boss what he had seen. McCarthy peered through the window himself and both men agreed that the Ripper had claimed another victim. They tried the door, but it was locked and McCarthy did not have a spare key, so McCarthy decided that the best course of action was to inform the police and had his man run to the Commercial Street police station, whilst he followed at a brisk walking pace. The police did not take much notice of the stammering Bowyer but took McCarthy much more seriously when he arrived at the station. Inspector Beck and his assistant Walter Dew accompanied the men back to Miller's Court and even though they were hardened police officers, they too were shocked by what they saw. Beck's first thought was to call for the bloodhounds and a short time afterwards the yard was filled with policemen. Inspector Abberline then arrived on the scene and was told by Beck that nobody had been into the room because they were awaiting the arrival of the dogs. The police had also called Dr George Bagster Phillips to the scene. Dr Phillips' immediate concern was to see if he could save the unfortunate's life, but after peering through the broken window decided that the room's occupant was long since dead. Dr Phillips then requested that the police officers bar access to the room until the bloodhounds arrived, so giving the dogs the best chance of picking-up the killer's scent. However, the bloodhounds were never to arrive. No one, not even the local police officers, knew of Sir Charles Warren's battles with the Home Secretary and the latter's department officials' neglecting to authorise the expenses for the dogs. So many hours were wasted whilst the officials awaited the arrival of the nonexistent animals. However, in the interim, the police were able to seal off the local area, take witness statements, search the yard for clues and question any suspicious looking men.

At 1.30pm Superintendent Arnold arrived. He informed Dr Phillips and the waiting police officers that the force no longer had access to the dogs and instructed his men to force open the door to Mary Jane's room. McCarthy was allowed into the room along with the policemen and Dr Phillips, and was soon back outside telling the inhabitants of Dorset Street about the sickening sight that had met his eyes. A shockwave of grief rippled through the people of the wicked quarter mile. The description of Mary Jane's murder went beyond what most of them were able to comprehend. There was none of the loud clamouring for news that took place following the murders of the previous victims and the tones of their conversations were hushed out of respect for the poor unfortunate who had been slaughtered by the hands of the Knife.

Abberline and Reid had already made-up their minds that if the maniac had not been caught in the act then he was never going to be caught. They had held out a faint hope that the bloodhounds would be able to follow the killer's footsteps through the city, but all hope was lost on Superintendent Arnold's arrival and the news about the dogs.

The press reported the murder in sombre sober tones, the sensationalist headlines were toned down and shorter, discreet stories were printed further into the newspapers. The articles relating to the earlier murders had made front-page news, many being two to three page extravaganzas; whereas, stories about Mary Jane's death were to be found on pages 5, 7, and 9. Even the inquest was completed in a single day with none of the long drawn out adjournments which had led to the soap opera type sagas of the previous victims' deaths.

Queen Victoria now took it upon herself to personally intervene in proceedings. Back in 1886, she had expressed her dissatisfaction with the police's ability to maintain public order in response to the protests of the unemployed. The Queen had gotten her wish when General Warren was brought in to lead the force and implemented structural changes along military lines. Such changes were beneficial in controlling public disorder, but did little to improve the detection of crime. Now a maniac was on the loose in her capital city and the recently reorganised police force did not appear to have the wherewithal to capture him. A day after Mary Jane's murder, the Queen sent a telegram to the Prime Minister, instructing that decided action must be taken to deal with the 'new most ghastly murder'. Three days later she was interrogating the Home Secretary on the minute details of the case. In 1886 Queen Victoria had informed her Prime Minister that she required a paramilitary police force; in the fall of 1888 she told him that she required a detecting police force.

The result of the Queen's intervention may have had unintended consequences. Only a year later the police would have to control strikers at London's docks. Warren's Force may well have broken the strike, but the force of 1889 was not able to do so. And so it is possible that the actions of the Ripper helped inadvertently to reverse some of the harsher conditions imposed upon London's poor during the early years of Queen Victoria's reign.

The Home Office responded to Mary Jane Kelly's murder by flooding the streets with even more policemen and Home Secretary Matthews even agreed for a special pardon to be granted specifically for any accomplice to Mary Jane Kelly's murder. In doing so, he had been careful not to admit any liability for not acting on Lusk's earlier request for a pardon following the murders of Stride and Eddowes.

A few days after Mary Jane's death Inspector Abberline was provided with the most vivid eye witness description of the entire murder investigation. A man named George Hutchinson, an out of work casual labourer, walked into a police station volunteering information about Kelly on the morning of her death, and was questioned directly by Abberline on 12 November. Hutchinson told Abberline that he had known Mary Jane for a number of years and that he was in the habit of giving her a few shillings to help her make ends meet. He described how he had spent Thursday in Romford, Essex, but had tramped back to London, arriving in Commercial Street at about 2.00am on the Friday morning. He said that he remembered passing a very well-dressed gentleman standing on the corner of Thrawl Street before encountering Mary Jane on the corner of Flower and Dean Street, where she asked if he could lend her sixpence, to which he replied that he could not let her have any money as he had spent everything that he'd had in Romford. Mary Jane was then to have said, 'I must go and look for some money' and starting walking toward Thrawl Street and the well-dressed man he had just passed. Hutchinson said that Mary Jane then propositioned the man and started leading him back to her room in 13 Miller's Court. Hutchinson added that ordinarily he would not have batted an eyelid about this, but on this occasion the man was so well-dressed that he thought there was something suspicious about the whole arrangement, so he followed Mary Jane and the man to Miller's Court and loitered outside the yard for about 45 minutes to check that all was well. At about 3.00am he even ventured as far as her room but as the light was off he decided to go to his lodgings and get some rest.

Inspector Abberline was the lead Detective Inspector in the case, had a wealth of experience of working in Whitechapel, and he believed the story that Hutchinson told him. As a result, he went on to write an official report including full details of Hutchinson's eyewitness statement. Hutchinson gave Abberline the most detailed description of any Ripper suspect, right down to the man's eyelids. Most noticeably of all, he stated that the man displayed from his waistcoat 'a massive gold chain, his watch chain having a big red seal, with a red stone, hanging from it'.

Nobody would ever come forward with any further details about Hutchinson's well-dressed foreign looking gentleman. I personally doubt that any such a man ever existed. There is one thing above all others that I find hard to accept about his story. All that I have read about life in Whitechapel indicates that Thrawl Street was slap bang in the middle of the wicked quarter mile, and was a street in which police officers feared to tread, walking through it in pairs for added security. For this reason alone, I find it very unlikely that a well-dressed man with a massive gold chain would hang around the corner of such a street at 2.00am. Such garb might have proven useful to a man like the

Ripper in attracting the attention of a poor unfortunate, but these women were rough and desperate, and many might not have thought twice about trying to rob a well-dressed toff. As for the police, they may have been very thin on the ground on the night before the Lord Mayor's show but I also have difficulty in believing that none of the officers on duty that night were able to remember seeing such a man. Even if they did not suspect him of being the Ripper, they must surely have expected him to get accosted by some of Whitechapel's less than savoury characters.

If Hutchinson's man was the Ripper, the implication is that the police were truly incompetent. Also it rules out the possibility of the Ripper having entered Mary Jane's room earlier that night. However, as already stated, Miller's Court was quite active that fateful night and neither Mrs Prater who lived directly above Mary Jane or Mrs Cox who lived further along the court saw or heard anything untoward until about 4.00am. If Mary Jane had been in and out of her lodgings all night with a string of clients, you would have expected someone else, in addition to George Hutchinson, to have seen or heard her and these other men. So I propose that Mary Jane entered her room at 11.45pm with a man with a large carroty moustache and was never again to step back out into the light of day.

Mary Jane Kelly's funeral took place on Monday 19 November. She was buried in St Patrick's Roman Catholic Cemetery, Leytonstone. Her coffin and burial plot were paid for by Henry Wilton, the Verger of St Leonard's church, who was determined that she would not be laid to rest in a pauper's grave. Thousands lined the streets as her coffin made its way to the cemetery. Mary Jane's birth had been celebrated by a few members of her family and their friends, she died at the hands of a maniac, and went to her grave mourned by thousands and was acknowledged by millions.

✤ ✤ ✤

It is the popular misconception that the authorities believed Kelly's murder to have been the last act of the Ripper. Home Office and Met Police files show that the authorities clearly did not think that the reign of terror had ended with Kelly's gruesome murder and a substantial number of extra officers, both uniformed and plain clothes remained on H Division's payroll until the end of February 1889. If Henry Wellcome was truly the Ripper he would in the weeks and months following Mary Kelly's death have either been planning his next murder or struggling with himself in a bid to end his reign of terror.

CHAPTER TWENTYTWO

He Snatched Defeat Out of the Jaws of Victory

By November of 1888 Henry Wellcome had become deeply immersed in arrangements for the new Burroughs Wellcome factory at Phoenix Mills, Dartford. The site was larger and allowed for greater possibilities than the limited space available at the existing factory in Wandsworth. Wellcome's relationship with Burroughs had started to improve somewhat as both men needed to work effectively together in order to facilitate smooth arrangements for the new factory. Rhodes James says that the two men worked together to make the Dartford site a model community, designed along the lines of Quaker families, the fine detail in their plans encompassing everything, even down to the design of the site's entrance gates. Therefore, at the end of 1888, the great stresses on Wellcome which had precipitated a four-month reign of terror were temporarily at an end. Rhodes James recorded that Wellcome wrote to his anxious mother to inform her that the worst had now passed in his life, that ultimate success seemed ensured, and that he was in good health and ready for the legal fray that lay ahead. So at the end of 1888 - the most stressful year in Henry Wellcome's life - he felt able to inform his mother that the worst was over and that he was back in control of events. Rhodes James provided further evidence of this using another of Wellcome's letters written by him in March 1889, addressed to a friend named Frank Lincoln. In the letter, Wellcome informed Lincoln of the great stresses that he had been under for the last two years, with enemies on all sides who were trying to wrest his business away from him. Wellcome added that he thought that these problems had arisen out of Burroughs' jealousy of him and the great position that he had achieved for himself in London society. He stated that both Burroughs and his wife were his sworn enemies. He went on to apologise to his friend for ignoring him for so long but then asked a favour at the end of the letter. Wellcome asked Lincoln to read his letter carefully, but then to burn it immediately, as he did not want his troubles known to the world.

I believe that Wellcome's letter to his friend Lincoln shows that early in 1889 Wellcome felt that he had spent two years in a great battle and finally felt confident of defeating his foes. He told his friend that all his troubles began through Burroughs' jealousy of his success, mentioning nothing about any of his own actions that may have caused a rift between him and his business partner; such as his advising Burroughs not to take Olive Chase as his wife or his poor time keeping at work. It is also worthy of note that that Wellcome requested his friend to 'burn' the letter after reading it. This shows Wellcome to be a very secretive and careful man, a man whose successes were clearly visible to all but whose true path through life would be made difficult to follow.

On 24 and 25 June 1889, legal matters finally came to a head when the case of Burroughs v. Wellcome came before Mr Justice Kekewich in the Chancery Division of the High Court. For all the trouble that Burroughs had gone to in taking Wellcome to court, including the smearing of Wellcome's name over the preceding months and years, Burroughs had not bothered to prepare witnesses from within the company to testify against his business partner. Burroughs was only able to call upon a lowly clerk named Prevost to testify against Wellcome. Whereas the forever organised Wellcome had witnesses which included the General Manager, (Sudlow), the Accountant and Assistant Manager (Kirby) and the Assistant Accountant (Spratlin). All that Prevost was able to do was reiterate Burroughs' assertion that since Wellcome's return from America, he would arrive for work most days after 11am, and leave sometime during the early afternoon.

Since the company accounts showed the business to be in good health, Mr Justice Kekewich ruled that there were no grounds for its dissolution. The judgement of the court was that: no such order of dissolution should be issued; that Wellcome should end his association with the publishing company Saxon and Company; and that court costs should be borne by both parties.

Wellcome telegraphed his mother immediately after the hearing with the message 'Victory'. Wellcome's future was now assured. He would bear stresses throughout the remainder of his eventful life, but none would affect him as greatly as the vice like grip he had felt under from 1887 to 1889.

Burroughs had lost the case and now would most likely have extreme difficulty in freeing himself from Wellcome's involvement in the company. However, he would take a revenge of sorts on his business partner, with devastating consequences for another of Whitechapel's poor unfortunate souls.

※ ※ ※

On 6 July 1889, only a few weeks after the court hearing, the Dartford factory was ready for its grand opening. Burroughs was a man born into wealth but had become obsessed with local politics and the inequities of life, and had even started rallying for free trade and against the ownership of land. He had been advocating the introduction of a land tax, a tax that would hit the purse strings of people just like himself, wealthy landowners. Wellcome also supported of free trade but was dead against the idea of a land tax. Wellcome did not care much for politics but many of his new wealthy friends did. They were Conservative in their politics and hated the idea of a land tax with a vengeance.

Burroughs appears to have become so obsessed with his radical politics, and let them take precedence over the grand opening of the new factory, with his planning on devoting the whole day over to speeches about land reform. Wellcome would have none of this and had the opening day split into two events, the afternoon dedicated to the formal opening of the factory, to be followed in the evening by a grand evening dinner. However, what actually happened on the day was to send the self-centred, narcissist Henry Wellcome into a rage. Burroughs highjacked the event by inviting a leading American socialist and advocate of land reform, Henry George, to be guest of honour at the grand opening. Rhodes James said that in spite of a Tory boycott, the day started well with two thousand guests walking around the grounds. However, Wellcome then noticed huge banners hailing not only Burroughs' guest of honour, which would have irked him as he would have wanted the day to revolve around himself, but also banners advocating Free Land. Wellcome did not attend the evening event, most probably because it became solely devoted to Henry George and Silas Burroughs and their speeches on free land and other socialist causes. The night time event was attended by the two thousand invited guests, together with about five thousand local people, many of whom had forced their way into the factory grounds; many others were only stopped from doing so by the presence of police with fire hoses, which they used as water cannons. The event ended with a firework display which included fire portraits which displayed the name of 'Henry George' and the slogan 'The Land for the People'. The event was enjoyed by all who attended it and went on until three in the morning.

To a megalomaniac self-publicist like Wellcome, being demoted to the sidelines by Burroughs in this way will have felt like a stab to the heart. On top of this, the event angered his rich friends and influential clients of the company who would have had huge misgivings about the public demonstration of the socialist leanings of the company. After the battles of the last two years, this would have been a huge and totally unexpected stressor in Wellcome's life, and I propose that he would have immediately reverted to type. It being likely that in the week following the grand opening of the new factory, that Wellcome would have arrived late to the office on several occasions, following a few late nights spent back in Whitechapel.

CHAPTER TWENTYTHREE

Alice McKenzie – One Last Hurrah

Alice McKenzie was about 40 years of age in 1889 and was a native of Peterborough. She was about 5 ft. 4 in. tall, was slim in build and had a fair complexion. Alice had moved to London's East End in about 1875 and met her long-term partner, a labourer named John McCormack, in 1882. In July of 1889, the couple's home was a common lodging house at 52 Gun Street, Spitalfields. Just like Liz Stride and Annie Chapman, Alice tried to make a living through charring, but was forced to make up for any shortfall in her earnings through prostitution. She was likely to have been addicted to both alcohol and tobacco and was known to drink to excess and smoke a pipe

On the afternoon of 16 July 1889, John McCormack returned to Gun Street following a hard day's work. He had woken early and was tired and wanted to catch some rest. He gave Alice 1s 8d in order to pay for their night's doss and other essentials, but before retiring to bed the couple had a row. Alice stormed out of the dosshouse with the money and McCormack being tired went to bed. Unbeknown to him, his words uttered to Alice in anger, would be last that he would ever say to her.

At about 7.00pm Alice took a blind boy, George Dixon, who also lived at the dosshouse to a local public house, the Royal Cambridge Music Hall. Whilst in the pub, Dixon heard Alice asking a man for a drink and his agreeing to buy her one. Shortly after that Alice took Dixon back to the dosshouse and made ready to go back out for the night. At about 8.30pm, and still quite early, she met the lodging house deputy, Elizabeth Ryder, who thought Alice to be in a state of inebriation. A few more hours passed and then at about 11.40pm, Alice bumped into a friend of hers, Margaret Franklin, on the front steps of a barber's shop on the corner of Brick Lane and Flower & Dean Street. Margaret tried to strike-up a conversation with Alice who was walking down the lane towards the Whitechapel High Street. Alice informed Franklin that everything was 'all right' adding that she 'can't stop now' and went hurriedly on her way.

֍ ֍ ֍

The Ripper was on the Whitechapel High Street. He had been back in his old haunts for the last few nights and had noticed the change in atmosphere; the streets were still filled with the poor and destitute, but the whores had lost their fear and he sensed that one of them would be ripe for the taking. A long time had passed since his last murder and he had a new plan. After the resurgence of slumming back in November of 1888, it had become fashionable for a man of means to frequent Whitechapel as a 'tourist' in the late hours of the evening and early hours of the morning. It was quite busy that night, but he reasoned that the police would take less notice of a lone man frequenting the area between twelve and one in the morning; as the pubs closed at 12.30am, when many a drunken man would spill out onto the streets. He was feeling a bit nervous, but fate was on his side as the weather was bad and it had been raining. So, along with many other men that unseasonably cold July night he was wearing a hat and a long dark coat. He had already chosen the time and location for his work, but now had to find a willing victim. He heard the church bells toll for 12am and prepared to make his move. He looked up and down the street in search of his prey from the whores who were making ready for the 12.30am rush. Then the whore with the pipe caught his eye. Yes, she would make for a fine night's work.

Alice had just lit her pipe when she saw the gentleman slummer looking her way. She asked him if he was seeking a bit of company and was taken a little by surprise at his American accent. They walked along the road, with her leading the way, but she sensed that the gent seemed to already know where they were going. Then he hesitated before finally agreeing to go up the narrow alley with her.

At 12.15am PC Joseph Allen, 423H, had taken a break from pounding his beat to eat a snack. The night had been quiet so far, but he expected it to get busier after the pubs closed. He stopped under the light of a street lamp in Castle Alley, a narrow street just off the Whitechapel High Street, and spent a few minutes eating his snack before going on his way. Just as PC Allen was departing the alley another PC, Walter Andrews, number 272H, entered it, arriving there at about 12.25am. All being well PC Andrews planned to return back there in twenty minutes time.

As PC Andrews made his way from Castle Alley into Old Castle Street a couple entered the alley from the Whitechapel High Street. Alice wanted to stay in the light and led the gent to the same street lamp where PC Allen had chosen to eat his snack. The Ripper had spent many months resisting the urge to kill and had hoped that he would never kill again, but he had not been able to stop himself. The urges flowed over him like waves and before he knew it he had found himself back in the wicked quarter mile, and now that he was back it felt like he had never been away. He did not much appreciate the whore's pipe, but it kept her busy as he surveyed the scene. He had been careful not to be seen entering the alley with her and he breezed through the gears of the trolling and wooing stages as he made ready to capture his prey. He wanted to see the terror in the whore's eyes when he took her, and in the blink of an eye his face changed from Jekyll's into Hyde's. Before the whore could scream the Ripper pounced, grabbing her around the throat and forcing her to the ground. She was still conscious when he pulled out his surgeon's knife and stabbed her twice in the left hand side of her neck. The wounds were wide enough and deep enough to kill her, but he'd held himself back from making the massive wounds that he'd inflicted on his past victims. He had changed; he still craved the planning, the chase and the capture; but his heart wasn't in it for the kill. As the whore lay dying in front of him he lifted her skirts and almost out of instinct, set to work on her. Just then it started to rain. Uncle Jacob had not had to work in the rain and this further ruined the moment for him. Then, as the Ripper hesitated, he heard the unmistakable sound of a policeman's hobnailed boots coming slowly up the alley. He quickly collected himself, left the whore where she lay and made his in the opposite direction, up the alley, into Old Castle Street and then away into the night.

***

It was about 12.50am when PC Andrews returned to Castle Alley. The pubs had closed now but luckily there had not been any trouble that he was aware of. He thought that people would not want to loiter in the rain and so he was expecting a quiet wet night ahead of him. Just then he saw a body lying close to a street lamp. When he got closer he could see blood flowing from the wounds in the left side of a woman's neck, that her skirts had been raised and her abdomen mutilated. Eight long months had passed since the slaughter of Mary Jane Kelly but PC Andrews was sure that the sight which met his eyes was the work of the Ripper. He blew on his police whistle and soon the alley was full of policemen.

At 3am James Monroe, the new Commissioner of the Metropolitan Police was in Castle Alley investigating the murder of a lowly, alcoholic, part-time prostitute. Monroe wanted to see the crime scene for himself and was later to write in a report to the Home Office that 'I am inclined to believe that the murder is identical with the notorious "Jack the Ripper" of last year'. Monroe must have believed what he had written, as later that same day he gave the order immediately to re-stablish plain clothes patrols in Whitechapel and increased the uniform strength of the district by an extra 22 men.

Inspector Reid was kept as busy as ever, but was to spend many wasted hours following-up what turned out to be a false confession to Alice's murder by a man named William Brodie.

Below is a map showing the location of Castle Alley relative to Commercial Street and the Whitechapel High Street.

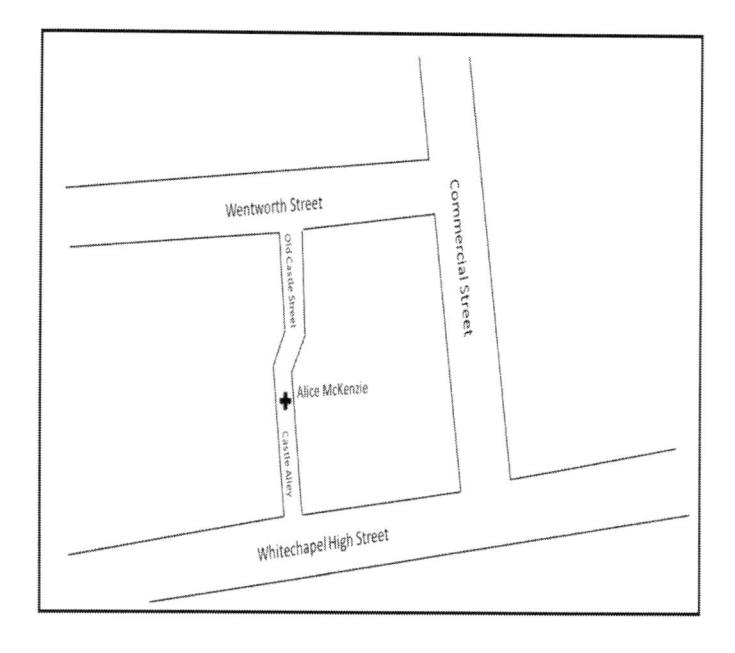

CHAPTER TWENTYFOUR

The Rise and Rise of Henry Wellcome

Wellcome finally recovered his composure following the debacle that was the Dartford Factory Opening Ceremony and he and Burroughs were able to work amicably for a few more months. However, before the year was out Burroughs would decide never to speak to directly to Wellcome again. Burroughs did not disclose the reason for the rift, but from then on, until his untimely death, the two men would only communicate with each other through their General Manager, Sudlow. In December 1894 the two men were again at loggerheads over ownership of the firm. Negotiations had been suspended when Burroughs started to become unwell. He appears to have been suffering from bronchitis and under advice from his doctor, took a break to the warmer climes of Monte Carlo to aid with his recovery. His condition was not to improve and in February 1895 Burroughs died from pneumonia.

Wellcome knew that Olive Burroughs hated him and now he was to go into battle with the woman he most likely considered to be the real cause of his rift with his long-time business partner. However, Wellcome was soon to have everything that he had strived so hard to achieve. His only setback that year was that one of his most trusted employees, friend and fellow Freemason, William Kirby, was to die in a tragic accident. In September 1895 Kirby was caught in an explosion caused by a gas leak in the kitchen of his home and died of his injuries a few days later.

The loss of Kirby aside, Wellcome now started to reshape the structure of his business. In 1894, he had persuaded Burroughs to allow the company to allocate some of its profits to research, with the establishment of a

Physiological Research Laboratory in the converted top floor of the Snow Hill headquarters. The laboratory was to specialise in the production of a diphtheria antitoxin. After Burroughs' death, Wellcome further promoted research and development into new products and encouraged eminent academics to work for the company. In 1896 he expanded the company's research facilities with the establishment of a Chemical Research Laboratory. The change in ethos paid dividends and over the years the company was to produce serum antitoxins, vaccines, anti-venoms, obstetric drugs and a range of veterinary products. The company also made major contributions to medical research, with pioneering work performed in such diverse fields, such as the study of adrenaline, histamine and malaria. By the late 1930s seventeen Burroughs Wellcome staff had become Fellows of the Royal Society, and one had received a Nobel Prize.

In 1897 Wellcome's mother died of breast cancer, she had been struggling valiantly against the illness for many years. In the eleven years before her death, Wellcome had only once travelled back to America to see her and the rest of his family. He had spent a lot of time in 1896 writing to her about his great litigation battles with Burroughs' widow Olive, who was opposed to his taking control of the company from her late husband. His mother knew that she was fading away and was only to receive letter after letter from her favoured son with reasons why he could not make the time to visit her. He is unlikely to have mentioned in any of these letters, that in the midst his great legal battles, he had somehow found the time to go sailing for a whole month in the English Channel. In the end he did not even find the time to go to her funeral. This understandably, was to cause a rift between him and his brother George.

The journey time from London to South Bend, Indiana, where Wellcome's mother had moved to, was about 11 days back in 1897. Not even a letter from his dying mother in which she wrote that it would be good if she could see him, would spur this man of great energy into making the trek to see her. However, by the time of his mother's death Wellcome most likely felt that he did not have need for anybody else; he was wealthy, probably beyond his wildest dreams, and had become a self-sufficient, self-made man of distinction.

Rhodes James is of the opinion that by 1897 Wellcome's conduct had begun to be dominated by his self-absorption and so uses this as an excuse for Wellcome not having anything to do with his dying mother and his not travelling to attend her funeral. However, one of the aims of this book has been to highlight any possible dysfunctional aspects in Wellcome's childhood and early life experiences that might have developed into a severe personality disorder. When viewed through this lens, Wellcome's relationship with his mother does not appear to have been a normal one. He appears to have been very keen to write to her with the details of his personal battles, and how he fought to achieve his personal success in life. But these letters can also be seen as his demonstrating to his mother that he had become a success in spite of his upbringing and not because of it. In short, there are indications that his relationship with his mother was not a good one.

CHAPTER TWENTYFIVE

Marriage, Travel, Sex and Curios

Wellcome's interest in artefacts started when he was only four years old. He was already collecting old medical paraphernalia in the late 1870s and continued to do so, as far as his budget would allow, during the 1880s. He had long since termed the items he collected as his 'curiosities' or 'curios'. Frances Larson in her book 'An Infinity of Things – How Sir Henry Wellcome Collected the World' has written that by 1880 a selection of his curiosities was deemed the finest display at that year's American Medical Convention. So whilst still relatively poor, Wellcome was most likely spending a significant proportion of his income on equipment and artefacts relating to medicine. It is my contention that Wellcome fed his addiction for collecting medical curios in order to try and crowd out fantasies relating to surgery that may have dogged him since childhood. However, if my theory is correct, then Wellcome would have found himself locked into a loop from which he would never be able to break free. With his buying items of medical equipment in an effort to divert himself from committing physical acts of surgery, only to feed his fantasies about performing surgery by the sight and touch of the new pieces of equipment, it is my assertion that such a vicious circle would tend over time to crowd out all other aspects of a person's life. Family, friends and work would all gradually have to take second place in such a person's fantasy filled mind.

In the mid 1890s Burroughs Wellcome and Co produced a diphtheria antitoxin from horses and in 1896 a sub-department was opened that produced thyroid and animal products. This work seems to have caught

Wellcome's imagination and he started spending much of his spare time researching the history of animal products in medicine. He started planning to write another book, this one to be entitled 'Animal Substances'. Frances Larson felt that Wellcome wanted to understand what drove human society to turn to animals in an effort to cure the physical ills in human beings. Larson wrote that about a year into his new project Wellcome realized that he would never be able to write the book alone, and as was his way, he recruited two experts, Charles John Samuel Thompson and Dr Friedrich Hoffman, to search out old books in Britain and Germany, for use in his research.

Work on the Animal Substances book led to Wellcome greatly expanding his private collection. He liked his library and now that he was a man of means, he decided in December 1899, to employ Thompson full-time as his collecting agent. The relationship between Wellcome and Thompson would be long lasting, with the two of them going on to work together for more than 25 years. The Animal Substances book never did materialize, but in 1913 Thompson would become curator of Wellcome's Historical Medical Museum. In the meantime Wellcome continued to scour antique shops in every country that he visited in the search of more medically related items for his ever expanding collection.

As a diversion from his work, late in 1889 Wellcome had taken to visiting his good friend Dr Thomas Barnardo, who by this time had moved from London's East End to a house close to the River Thames, at St Leonard's Lodge, Surbiton. Barnardo may have spent his days working for the destitute children of London but his family enjoyed a comfortable living. This might go some way to explaining why Barnardo's wife, preferred to be known as the 'Begum', a title used by wives of an Aga. That said, it must be added that Dr Barnardo was a genuinely religious man, insisting on his family saying prayers every day, with his children learning to recite passages from the bible. By all accounts this made for a quite stifling family atmosphere when he was at home with them. As for the Begum, she had grand plans for her daughter, Gwendoline Maude Syrie Barnardo, who liked to be called 'Queenie', but was also comfortable with plain old 'Syrie'. The Begum had steered her daughter away from unsuitable matches of marriage and appears to have decided that only a man of wealth and distinction would be good enough for her little Queenie. So when the now very wealthy 47 year old American born Henry Wellcome started frequenting the family home, she was determined to make a match with him for her 21 year old daughter.

Wellcome was known to enjoy the company of women but apart from Burroughs' hint that he may have spent his time with 'gay' women; there was no sign of any potential Mrs Wellcome before he started making regular trips to the Barnardo home. Wellcome rented a house close to that of Barnardo and his family, and used it as a base for his canoeing outings on the river. However, even then, Wellcome was not known to have gone beyond attending family picnics and taking Syrie and her brothers out for boating trips on the river.

Wellcome had a keen interest in Africa and became involved with Lord Kitchener after donating 100 guineas in response to Kitchener's public appeal to build a college at Khartoum in memory of General Gordon, a man killed at the hands of the Mahdi's forces in 1895. It turned out that Kitchener had read Wellcome's book on the Metlakahtlan Indians and this greatly increased Wellcome's interest in Kitchener's work in the Sudan and led to his donating medical equipment and stock to the college's dispensary. In the autumn of 1900 Wellcome sailed to Cairo and went on to study the conditions of the native peoples of the Sudan. Wellcome found the climate in the Sudan to his liking and beneficial to his health, and so decided to establish a tropical research laboratory in the country's second largest city, Khartoum.

By all accounts, Syrie Barnardo appears to have been a wily gold digger. This is very much evident in Selina Hastings book 'The Secret Lives of Somerset Maugham'. Syrie and her mother appear to have hatched a plan to ensnare Wellcome, and so it was that when Wellcome made a return trip to Cairo, a large party of English ladies arrived there at the same time; one of these ladies just happened to be Syrie Barnardo. Hastings implies in her book that later in life Syrie would entrap the world famous writer Somerset Maugham into marriage by getting pregnant. Gerald McKnight wrote a book in which she implies that the same trick might even have been tried on Henry Wellcome. In 'The Scandal of Syrie Maugham', McKnight hints that the couple rushed into marriage, without even waiting for Dr Barnardo's blessing. The implication is that Syrie might also have gotten pregnant before her marriage to Wellcome. However, if this is the case, she must have miscarried, as she was not to bear a child by him until 1903.

All that can be said with any certainty is that the couple quickly became engaged and were married at St Mark's Church in Surbiton, within ten days of returning to England, on 25 June 1891. Notably, Syrie's father Dr Barnardo did not return to England from Germany for his daughter's wedding; he had by that time a weak heart and was at that time recovering from an attack of angina. However, one can only guess at how Dr Barnardo may have felt if he had actually walked his 21 year old daughter down the church aisle and into the arms of her soon to be husband, a man 26 years her senior and only seven years his junior.

The newlyweds moved into a rented house, the Oast House at Hayes in Kent. It is likely that Syrie anticipated living the remainder of her life in luxury; throwing lavish parties and staying in the most expensive of hotels, whilst travelling to the world's most exotic locations. In all this, Syrie was to be proved entirely wrong.

As for Wellcome, he had finally been 'buckled', and so hopefully, the potentially uncontrollable urges of the late 1880s would be laid to rest forever. He would now keep his wife constantly by his side. He now had two passions that would help quell his lust for surgery, his wife and his collecting. It would soon become clear which of the two passions would take the greater precedence in his affections, and it was not to be his wife.

Syrie was to find that indeed, her new husband liked to travel the world, but he tended not to visit lavish locations, and instead was quite happy touring poor disease ridden lands where he could study the effects of illness on the local people's malnourished bodies. Tours to Europe were no more enjoyable for Syrie, as Henry was obsessed with the newly invented motorcar. Wellcome drove the couple many hundreds of miles over bumpy roads in his breakdown prone vehicle. When they finally did get to their destination, he was off dragging his bride around old antiques shops in his obsessive search for more curiosities to add to his burgeoning collection. Syrie informed her friends that following her marriage, she was travelling to places that she detested and that she derided her husband's curios. She had left her father's house with its stifling atmosphere of adherence to religious worship, to spend hours in the company of staid, serious minded academic men and their wives. In short, she was unhappy with her lot in life.

However, what is of far greater interest to me and has a bearing on the events of 1888 is that Wellcome's wife was also unhappy because of the suggestion of his physical treatment of her. Having likely married Wellcome for his money and status, it was improbable that she would ever divulge publicly anything against him. However, Syrie is said to have confided in her closest friends and they would go on to tell tales about how the hugely successful Henry Wellcome allegedly treated his wife. McKnight relates that one of Syrie's best friends, Dame Rebecca West, claimed that from all that she had heard about Wellcome, there appeared to be a streak of sadism in him. Dame Rebecca said that she had been told by several people, including Ronald Storrs (T.E. Lawrence's great friend) that Wellcome had been frightfully cruel to Syrie, allegedly beating Syrie with something called a Sjamsok – a heavy leather whip - which he brought back from his overseas travels. McKnight included comments made by an ex-member of Wellcome's staff, a man named John Camp. Camp stated that a source close to Wellcome had informed him that Wellcome had disgusted his wife with his sexual demands and that Syrie had rejected Wellcome utterly in their final years together. Camp may have had many reasons for spreading such rumours, but I feel that rumours such as these would be regarded as unusual if spread about a man living in modern times, by twentyfirst century internet trolls, let alone by the more prudent Victorian citizens of the 1890s.

Further fuel to these rumours of Wellcome's sadistic tendencies was added by the MP Horatio Bottomley, the then editor of the John Bull magazine, a periodical known for publicly attacking many notable figures of the age. Bottomley is said to have unearthed accounts of Wellcome's cruel behaviour whilst away in North Africa. One of the rumours being spread about Wellcome was that if he ever caught a guard sleeping whilst on duty around his camp, he would take it upon himself to personally beat the man. These rumours appear to have culminated in a libel action that was settled out of court. Such stories are repeated in Hastings' book, where she states that Syrie made no complaints about Wellcome during her marriage, but later confided to one or two intimates of her distaste for Wellcome's sexual demands; hinting of beatings, brutality, sadistic tendencies and pain inflicted in the bedroom. Hastings made further comments that it was fortunate for Syrie's peace of mind that she would have not have heard the rumours - involving the savage flogging of native bearers and of a child strung up by its feet and whipped until it died - until after she had separated from him. I have also found comments made on the website (www.briandeer.com) by a British Investigative Reporter and Sunday Times journalist, Brian Deer, in which Mr Deer informed in an article of 19 September 1993 entitled 'Sir Henry Wellcome – thy will be done' that reasons included in Sir Henry's marriage break-up with Syrie included Wellcome's 'peculiarities' getting on her nerves. Mr Deer wrote in the article that one of Wellcome's habits included running into her room, wearing nothing but a raincoat before throwing it off and jumping in her bed. The source of Mr Deer's information appears to have come from either a contemporary press comment or a leak from a secret biography of Wellcome held by the Wellcome Trust.

Now all of the this can be classed as simple hearsay, with the alleged beatings and alleged sexually sadistic behaviour not inevitably replacing the evisceration of fallen woman in Whitechapel. Nevertheless, the rumours all point to Wellcome being a potentially violent, possibly sexually deviant man, who might acquaint sexual activity with the wearing of a raincoat, and who also might be capable of inflicting savage beatings on those who he deemed deserved them.

CHAPTER TWENTYSIX

Separation and Divorce

Wellcome's marriage was not a happy one and his relationship with Syrie was not improved by the birth of his son, Henry Mounteney Wellcome, on 26 June 1903. After Mounteney's birth, Henry continued to travel all over the country and the world in the same manner as he had done before. Syrie had found travel uncomfortable before the birth of her son and she was certainly not going to find it any easier with a babe in arms. In addition to the labours of travelling, when Wellcome staged a major event, he did as he had always had done and controlled all the significant arrangements himself and wanted to be the centre of attention. This effectively gave Syrie nothing of significance to do. Rhodes James informs that even for Mounteney's christening party, Wellcome planned and organised everything himself, so ensuring that he was the central figure on the day. The final strain on the relationship probably came from their infant child. It soon became apparent that Mounteney had learning difficulties and although there is no any evidence that either parent loved their child any the less for this, it is unlikely to have made life any easier for the recently married couple.

So over time Syrie appears to have become tired and bored with her life with Wellcome. In September 1909, Wellcome was again suffering one of his frequent bouts of ill health, so the couple sailed for New York, travelling from there to the dry climes of California so that Henry could indulge in some rest and recuperation. It is thought that the couple were not on the best of terms and spent a lot of time quarrelling. Whilst in America, Wellcome became sidetracked by a request from the American authorities to go to

Panama to perform an independent assessment on the health and sanitary conditions of workers involved in the building of the Panama Canal. The couple detoured to Quito, Ecuador; where the plan was for Wellcome to leave Syrie with some American friends whilst he went on alone to inspect the Panama Canal Zone. Also staying in Quito was a 50 year old wealthy American railroad builder and financer, Archer Harman. Details are sparse, but Wellcome was to accuse Syrie of being unfaithful with Harman. The couple had furious rows and depending on whose version of events you believe, Syrie either fled the scene in fear of her life or stormed off angrily to New York. Whether they knew it or not at the time, the couple were never to see each other in a social setting again and effectively remained separated until they formally divorced on 14 February 1916.

Wellcome did not follow his wife to try and save their marriage; instead he stayed in the Americas and completed his inspection of the Panama building zone, his assessment being well received by the American government. He later returned to England and formalised terms for his separation from Syrie, ensuring that their financial arrangements gave him a controlling interest in the upbringing of his son.

Syrie was to want for nothing as Wellcome had provided her with a generous annual allowance. She appears to have had a number of relationships with wealthy men, including Gordon Selfridge, who may have bought her a house in London. Eventually she met a man that she fell in love with, a young successful writer by the name of Somerset Maugham. Syrie appears to have trapped Maugham into marriage by deliberately getting pregnant and even though Maugham had predominantly homosexual tendencies the couple agreed to marry. However, at the time of the birth of their baby girl, Liza, Syrie was still married to Wellcome. Wellcome does not appear to have had a problem with remaining married to Syrie and few people in his professional world even knew that he even had a son.

However, Wellcome would have been aware that his having a second child, fathered by another man, was not a situation that peers in his social and business circles would find acceptable. So with right now clearly on his side, he filed for divorce. Wellcome's private investigators and divorce lawyers supposedly provided him with evidence against two men as being possible fathers to Syrie's second child. The other man was the wealthy department store owner, Gordon Selfridge. However, true to the Masonic code, Wellcome filed for divorce citing Maugham as the adulterer, as Gordon Selfridge was not only a fellow Mason but was also a member of Wellcome's own Masonic Lodge.

Syrie's second marriage was also a tumultuous affair and was most likely to have been doomed even before it started. The couple had no other children and were eventually to separate and divorce. Syrie had never been slow in making the best for herself and went on to work as a very successful interior designer, meeting with equal success in Britain and America.

Wellcome went on to become richer and more successful, but he was never to remarry and by all accounts turned into a lonely miserable man.

My speculation on Wellcome's life after his separation from Syrie is that he would have been raging with anger, and this is very likely to have resulted in the return to behaviours exhibited in 1888-89. If this is the case, then at least one Ripper style murder should have taken place close to the camps that Wellcome stayed at whilst performing his inspections relating to the works of the Panama Canal. However, I have not found any evidence of any such murders being committed. By the time he finally returned to England, the stress and anger felt by his conviction in his wife's adultery should have abridged, enabling him to carry on with a regular life. I have not been able to find any evidence of any gruesome murders of poor or fallen women in the Americas or elsewhere in the world, but one can wonder if the rumoured brutal horse whipping of the poor camp guards might have served to satisfy the blood lust of our likely sadistic serial murderer?

JOSEPH BUSA

CHAPTER TWENTYSEVEN

Honours and His Legacy

Wellcome renounced his American citizenship in 1905 and on 1 November 1910 he was to commit himself to Great Britain, taking British Citizenship by making an Oath of Allegiance to His Majesty King George V. Like most people of greatness, he set about creating his legacy as he passed into old age. In June 1913, in his 60th year, he finally displayed a selection of his massive collection of medical artefacts in his Historical Medical Exhibition. Later that summer, the exhibition was turned into the Wellcome Historical Medical Museum. In 1924 Burroughs' name was lost to history with Wellcome's consolidation of all his business interests into The Wellcome Foundation Limited, for which he was the sole shareholder. This new private company included his worldwide pharmaceutical business, research laboratories and his massive collection of curios. In 1932, in his 79th year, Henry Solomon Wellcome became Sir Henry Solomon Wellcome. Sir Henry, his status as a great British citizen assured, wrote a will in which he established The Wellcome Trust, the body that would represent him after his death.

As part of the celebration of the 75th anniversary of the creation of The Wellcome Trust, the Trust commissioned a book into Sir Henry's life, many great achievements and his legacy. The book written by J.A. Flannery and K.M. Smith is called 'Sir Henry Wellcome – Backwood to Knighthood', contains an observation that goes furthest to mirroring my own thoughts and theories about Wellcome's life. I am unable to provide an actual quote. However, an opinion expressed by the authors is that even though Henry became the esteemed Sir Henry in 1932, he was to receive another honour in March of that year that would have filled him with even greater pride. That honour was his being made an Honorary Fellow of the Royal College of Surgeons.

I can only agree wholeheartedly with such an observation. Because, if what I have written is true, no greater honour could have been bestowed upon man that I believe to have been Jack the Ripper!

EPILOGUE

Sir Henry Wellcome' funeral took place on 30 July 1936 at Golder's Green Crematorium, where his body was cremated. The next day the urn containing his ashes was delivered to his Historical Medical Museum, where it was catalogued and placed in the strong room alongside some of his most precious curios. His ashes were finally retrieved from his collection and were buried in the churchyard of St Paul's Cathedral in February 1987, with a commemorative plaque being placed in the church's crypt.

My hypothesis has been that Sir Henry Wellcome spent much of his life trying to control the two dogs of his personality; the mad evil one that dreamed of surgery and death, and the good one intent on living a good life and curing the ills of his fellow man. I believe that he tried to control his dark side through his obsession with collecting and through his marriage. However, during the period from 1888 to 1889, in the midst of his legal battle with Silas Burroughs, his dark side held sway, and resulted in the violent death of six fallen women of Whitechapel.

If all this is true, then somewhere hidden in plain sight, amongst the million plus items of his curios, will have been a few cheap brace rings and some specimen jars containing women's body parts of unknown origin. Over the years, many items will have been destroyed, sold or lent to other museums for their own displays. But if such items do exist, then there remains the faintest of chances that modern science could one day be used to finally lay the ghost of the Ripper to rest.

Now if you have read this far, it is clear that I have been unable to find the smoking gun proving that Sir Henry Wellcome was in fact Jack the Ripper. However, as I wanted to make clear from the start, the primary aim of this book is to rouse the interest of better minds than my own into making a forensic study into Sir Henry Wellcome's life, viewed not through the rose tinted glasses previously afforded to such a great man, but through the lens of the long past detectives of the Ripper Unit.

Many people have no doubt already made the trip to 183 Euston Road and viewed a free exhibition entitled 'Medicine Man' located on the first floor of the Wellcome Trust's grand building. For those of you who have not done so, I suggest that you go and see what I have seen. Now I am sure that you are already thinking that you can view all there is to see on the internet. But trust me on this, if you view the images on the net, you will truly be looking without seeing. Only if you make the journey and look at the surgical knives, the implements of torture, the death masks and most of all Nezzo's painting of a man grabbing a woman's chin whilst hiding a surgical implement behind his back; will you really be able decide if you have seen into the mind of a serial murderer, a murderer that went by the trade name of Jack the Ripper.

APPENDIX

The Usual Suspects

Many men's names have been put forward as being responsible for the Whitechapel murders. Notably, Sir Henry Soloman Wellcome is not one of them. There are good reasons for this, including that: he did not live or work in Whitechapel, he had no proven record of violence against women or men, he was a very successful businessman and he was not thought prone to mental illness. However I hope that, as I have sought to demonstrate, far more interest needs be shown into the motives and actions of this great man, examining whether Wellcome's upbringing and life experiences up to and including 1888 match the basic profile of a serial killer.

Over time the real experts in the field have uncovered a number of other prime suspects. I have summarised details of these men for comparison with Sir Henry Wellcome and hope that after reading about them you will agree that Wellcome more than deserves his place in any modern day line-up.

George Chapman

As a result of DNA testing organised by the businessman Russell Edwards in 2014, there can be no disputing that George Chapman is at this time of writing the man thought most likely to be the Ripper. However, although I have not read Mr Edwards' book 'Naming Jack the Ripper: New Crime Scene Evidence, A Stunning Forensic Breakthrough, The Killer Revealed', I'm content to stick with my original view on the likelihood or not of Chapman being our killer.

Severin Klosowski was born in Poland, where he qualified as a junior surgeon in 1887. In late 1887 or early 1888 he arrived in London and found work as an assistant hairdresser. He met a lady named Lucy Baderski and the couple were married in October 1889. In 1890 he was working in a barber's shop in the basement of the White Hart pub in George Yard, the same road on which Martha Tabram met her death. The couple left London for Jersey City in America in 1891 where Severin also found work as a barber. The couple had a stormy relationship and a pregnant Lucy returned to England where she had a baby girl on 15 May 1892. A few months later the couple were reunited in London but the marriage was not to last, with their finally separating for good in 1893 when Severin found another woman, named Annie Chapman. Severin and Annie soon parted company but by this time Severin must have been more confident of his command of the English language and took on the name of George Chapman.

George found another lady friend named, Mary Spink, whom he might also have married. This relationship was also not to last as Mary died on Christmas Day 1897. Not wasting much time, George met and married another woman, Bessie Taylor, but she too died early into the relationship on 13 February 1901. By now one suspects that any woman aware of Chapman's past might be wary of getting overly involved with him but he was soon to meet and marry yet another lady, Maud Marsh. However, when Maud died on 22 October 1902 her family, who might have been aware of Chapman's past, sought the medical opinion of their own doctor into her death. The doctor did find something suspicious and as result permission was granted to exhume the bodies of Chapman's two most recent wives. Even though the bodies must have been badly decomposed, significant amounts of poison were found inside what was left of them. On this evidence Chapman was found guilty of murdering three of his wives, given the death sentence and was executed in Wandsworth Prison on 7 April 1903.

The sales of newspapers must have increased for a while whilst the press reported the gory details of Chapman's crimes, conviction and execution. However, not slow to find further headline grabbing stories, a journalist from the Pall Mall Gazette decided to seek the opinion of the policeman most intimately involved in the Ripper case, Frederick Abberline, who by now was enjoying his retirement from the force. This turned out to be a clever move on the part of the journalist, as Abberline said that he himself had been 'so struck with the coincidences in the two series of murders' that he had not been able to 'think of anything else for several days past'. Abberline added that 'there are a score of things which make one believe that Chapman is the man'. All these quotes are likely to have convinced the general public at the time that the police had finally gotten their man.

Since Chapman was already dead, it was not possible for the police to question him about the Ripper murders. So we are left with a man who had an interest and knowledge of surgery, was in London at the times of the Whitechapel murders and had been confirmed to be a serial murderer. For these reasons a significant number of Ripperologists quite rightly believe that Chapman cannot be discounted as the murderer. However, there are two question marks against his being the Ripper. Firstly, knowing that he was going to his death in a very public way, why would he not admit to the Ripper murders? This could have served to boost his ego or at least clear his conscience. Secondly, the modus operandi (MO) of the murders was different. As informed earlier, serial murderers have specific MOs that fulfil their fantasies. They enjoy killing in a certain way, so it would have been very unusual (but not impossible) for Chapman to have committed two very different types of serial murder. I think for both these reasons, it is unlikely that Chapman was the Ripper.

Thomas Cutbush

Thomas Hayne Cutbush was the nephew of a senior Metropolitan Police Officer, Executive Superintendent Charles Cutbush. Important family relations aside; Thomas was a lunatic and was detained in London's Lambeth Infirmary on 5 March 1891. However, he escaped from the infirmary on the day of his detention and whilst at large stabbed a lady named Florence Johnson and attempted to stab another. Cutbush was arrested on 9 March 1891. This time no chances were taken in regard to his mental health and he was declared insane in April of that year and sent to the maximum security Broadmoor Criminal Lunatic Asylum.

Although Cutbush was literally a knife welding maniac and had been a serious a threat to the women of London, he might easily been forgotten in the sands of time but for his relationship to his uncle Charles. The Sun newspaper picked up the story as they clearly thought that there could be a serious connection with the Whitechapel murders, but were wary of naming an individual with family connections to a senior member of the Police Service. On 13 February 1894 the newspaper started publishing articles stating that it knew the identity of Jack the Ripper, but no mention was made of the suspect's name. The sensationalist articles started to rekindle public interest in the Whitechapel murders and the authorities became worried that it would look like the police had not only failed to catch the Ripper at the time of the Whitechapel murders but were now covering-up his identity in an effort to project the Force's reputation. Finally the Chief Constable of Scotland Yard, Sir Melville Leslie Macnaghten produced a report refuting the Sun's claims. Although unable to account for Cutbush's whereabouts on the nights of the murders, Macnaghten was able to highlight errors in the Sun's stories. The intervention by such a senior ranking official was enough to put the matter to rest, with the Sun newspaper and its readership again losing interest in the unsolved murders. So we are able to rule out Cutbush on the grounds that a senior Metropolitan Police Officer had provided evidence against his being the Ripper. If the police did not think him likely to have committed the murders, then who has the authority to argue against their judgement?

Sir Melville's document was temporarily lost to the sands of time until it was discovered by Ripperologists searching for new clues into the Ripper's identity in the late 1950s. The document, which became known as the Macnaghten Memorandum, included the names of three other men (Montague John Druitt, Aaron Kosminski and Michael Ostrog) of which Macnaghten wrote 'any one of whom would have been more likely than Cutbush to have committed the series of murder'.

Macnaghten's Memorandum has been treated seriously by Ripperologists because although he did not join the force until 1889, he had access to the officers and files relating to the case. Also, two of the three men (Druitt and Kosminski) included in his report did not become suspects until after he had taken up his post at the Yard, so he was likely to have access to original reports at the time that they were written by the investigating officers.

Just as an aside, Charles Cutbush also suffered from mental illness. He ended his life in March 1896, committing suicide by shooting himself in the head whilst in the company of his daughter Ellen.

Montague John Druitt

As already mentioned, Montague Druitt was not suspected of being a Ripper suspect back in 1888-89. Druitt was a barrister who also worked as a schoolmaster at Mr George Valentine's boarding school in Blackheath. He did not have direct medical knowledge but did come from a family of doctors, so he is more likely than most to have had an understanding of anatomy and the human body. There is absolutely no proof that Druitt was violent in any way or that he visited Whitechapel at the time of the murders. Macnaghten included Druitt in the list of suspects for two main reasons. Firstly, because Druitt's family had informed the police of their suspicions that he might be the killer and, being doctors, their opinion was likely to have been taken much more seriously than those of the average member of the public. Secondly, Druitt committed suicide by drowning himself in the River Thames sometime in November 1888. The theory was that it was possible that he could not live with himself after committing the horrendous murder of Mary Jane Kelly. So, if there really were no further Ripper murders after November 1888, it was possible that they had stopped because the perpetrator Druitt had killed himself.

In light of the lack of proof of Druitt's guilt ever being passed onto the police by his family, we only have hearsay evidence against him. This is hardly a good reason for Macnaghten to have selected Druitt as a more likely Ripper than Thomas Cutbush, let alone Druitt being the police's choice as the primary suspect for the Whitechapel murders. Also, there are suspicions that Druitt was a homosexual, in which no way rules him out as a possible murderer, but in the world of sexual serial killers, the tendency is for heterosexual men to murder women and for homosexual men to murder other men. Therefore, if Druitt was homosexual then not only would he have been one of the world's first recognized serial killers, but he would have been a deviant one at that. This makes the case against him quite difficult to believe.

Suspicions about Druitt's sexuality arose because shortly before he committed suicide he was dismissed from the boys school in which he was a teacher. The rather unspecific reason of 'serious trouble' was given for his dismissal, the phrase likely as not to have been a euphemism for homosexual activities with a boy or boys.

Druitt's brother William produced a letter addressed to him from Montague that included the line 'Since Friday I felt I was going to be like mother, and the best thing for me was to die'. William informed the inquest into Druitt's death that their mother had become insane the previous July. Although not being an expert on mental health, I cannot rule out that Montague Druitt would have associated activities like savagely murdering five prostitutes with his 'going to be more like mother', but I find it very hard to believe that she had set a benchmark of madness that Jack the Ripper had yet to reach.

Sir William Gull

Sir William Gull, Physician-in-Ordinary to Queen Victoria and a senior Freemason has been proposed as being central to a plot to protect the British Establishment and the Royal Family from scandal.

The theory has it that Prince Albert Victor, Duke of Clarence, grandson to Queen Victoria, eldest son of Albert Edward and so Heir Presumptive to the throne; is supposed to have fallen in love with a shop assistant, a Catholic commoner named Annie Elizabeth Crook, resulting in consequences for some of Whitechapel's fallen class. The prince is said to have become infatuated with Annie and secretly married her after making her pregnant; with Mary

Jane Kelly witnessing their marriage ceremony. Over time the secret got out and the then Prime Minister, Lord Salisbury, is supposed to have sanctioned a plan to hush-up the marriage. Lord Salisbury and/or other members of the Establishment supposedly arranged for Annie's shop to be raided and for her to be removed to a secure asylum for the rest of her life, with Prince Albert Victor being removed from the public eye and eventually taken out of the country to India. However, the theory has it that the authorities supposedly missed the child, who had been placed in the care of Mary Jane Kelly. Kelly then realising that her life might be in danger, is said to have left the child in the care of a gentleman named Walter Sickert and fled to the East End of London, where she hoped to lose herself in the somewhat lawless wicked quarter mile. Whilst 'safely' hidden away in the rookeries of Whitechapel, Mary Jane is thought to have told a group of prostitutes her tale and they then encouraged her to blackmail the British Government into paying her to keep quiet about the whole affair.

The story continues with Sir William Gull having accepted the mission of saving the Royal Family and the Establishment from embarrassment and instability. Gull is said to have selected the assistance of the Deputy Commissioner of the Metropolitan Police, Dr Robert Anderson, and a coachman named John Netley, in his plan to save the nation. Details of the story were provided by a painter, come actor, Walter Sickert. Sickert is said to have unburdened his soul to his son Joseph shortly before his death, telling him full details of the plot.

The story goes that Sir William and Netley killed all the prostitutes who knew about the marriage and the child. Dr Robert Anderson is said to have located the fallen women for them and helped to cover their tracks after the gruesome assaults. Sir William being a senior Freemason, supposedly chose to kill the fallen woman in accordance with the ritual methods allegedly reserved for traitors of the

Brotherhood.

My comment on this is that if these women really realised that they were being systematically rounded-up and murdered, they would have told their stories to all and sundry in an effort to save their lives; something they do not appear to have tried to do. If the reason for their murder was really to silence a group of blackmailers, then the need to silence them would have greatly diminished after their secret was made public.

George Hutchinson

Hutchinson was a casual labourer, who lived and worked in Whitechapel at the time of the murders.

I have included Hutchinson in my list of suspects as the Ripperologist, John J. Eddleston choose him as his most likely Ripper suspect in his book 'Jack the Ripper – An Encyclopaedia'. As we already know, Hutchinson provided Inspector Abberline with the eyewitness description of a well-dressed man who supposedly picked up Mary Jane Kelly at about 2am on the morning of her murder at 13 Miller's Court.

I personally do not believe Hutchinson's story of a well-dressed, moneyed individual loitering around Thrawl Street at 2am in the morning. Even if the man had been the Ripper, he would have had as much trouble trying to evade robbers as he would the police. Most people should have found Hutchinson's description of the killer hard to believe, on the grounds that such an obviously well to do man could not have waltzed through Whitechapel's streets over the period of a few months, without anyone other than Hutchinson seemingly giving him a second glance.

However, I would not want to rule him out as being a strong suspect for the Ripper, as his home base was at the centre of the crime scenes, with Hutchinson's lodgings being located very much where a geographical profiler would have expected the Ripper to have lived. Also, if Hutchinson was the Ripper, it is highly likely that he was loitering in Miller's Court at about 2.30am, when another eyewitness, Sarah Lewis, says that she saw a man at the front of the court, who looked like he was waiting for someone. So it is possible that Hutchinson panicked when he discovered that Sarah Lewis had seen someone and wanted to provide the police with the description of a fictitious suspect to help cover-up his own tracks.

Aaron Kosminski

The second man named in the Macnaghten Report was that of a Polish Jew named Aaron Kosminski. Kosminski was a feeble-minded man, who would now be classed as having learning difficulties. It is thought that in all his time in England he never managed to get to grips with the language and rarely spoke English. Whitechapel had a large Jewish Community, so he was able to get through life speaking in his native language, Yiddish. During the late 1880s, Kosminski gradually went insane, he was thought likely to have been schizophrenic, and believed that his actions were being controlled by higher powers. Although a man without any means of support, he refused any charity offered to him, instead choosing to eat food from the gutter.

Macnaghten in his report wrote that 'This man became insane owing to many years of indulgence in solitary vices. He had a great hatred of women, especially of the prostitute class, and had strong homicidal tendencies'. Now if all this is true and we have no reason not to believe it to be so, then Kosminski shows some of the classic signs of the fall into the serial killing madness. The euphemism 'indulgence in solitary vices' clearly referred to excessive masturbation.

So he may also have had violent sexual fantasies about women. However, Kosminski would certainly have had no access to any sort of pornography, so in no way would he have seen visual images that might have helped him along the deviant path of sexual murder.

Kosminski was clearly mad and a danger to the public and was admitted to the Colney Hatch Asylum in February 1891. A few years later in 1894 he was transferred to Leavesden Asylum where he died in 1919. It is interesting to note that during the entire period of his confinement, Kosminski was never classed as homicidal and was not considered a danger to others.

However, Kosminski although only second on Macnaghten's list of the three most likely Ripper suspects, was supposedly positively identified by an eyewitness as being the man seen with one of the Whitechapel murder victims just before her death. It is thought that this witness was either Joseph Lawende, in the case of Catherine Eddowes, or Israel Schwartz in the case of Elizabeth Stride. The man was taken to view Kosminski sometime during 1890, two years after the murders. However, as both the witness and Kosminski were Jewish, it is believed that the witness having made the positive identification, then refused to give evidence in a court of law as he realised that Kosminski would most likely receive the death penalty, with his religious beliefs not permitting him to help condemn another man to death. So, the police with their hands tied, are said to have placed Kosminski under surveillance whilst gathering enough evidence to have him classed as insane and locked away for the rest of his life in mental institutions.

My view on Kosminski's inclusion in Macnaghten's list is this. The women murdered by the Ripper were clearly manoeuvred into going into secluded locations with him. In several instances this was way past 1am when the streets would have become particularly deserted. I have great trouble in visualising how a beggar in drab dress and possessing a very poor command of the English language, could have approached and sweet talked women into going into dark secluded spots where he could then savagely murder them. Even by the standards of the wicked quarter mile, he would have most likely been dressed in rags and would clearly not have had a penny to his name. I think that even a low class prostitute desperate for her doss money would have confronted any man who approached her, if it looked highly unlikely that he possessed the 4d required for her services.

Michael Ostrog

The third man named by Macnaghten was Michael Ostrog (aka Bertrand Ashley, Dr Barker, Stanislas Lublinski and Count Sobieski amongst many others). Ostrog was referred to as a 'Russian doctor, whose antecedents were of the worst type and his whereabouts at the time of the murders could not be ascertained'. It was claimed that he was 'habitually cruel to women' and that he 'carried about with him surgical knives'.

Ostrog appears to have been a professional criminal, working as a high-class con artist, who spent many years of his adult life in prison. When Ostrog arrived in England, he was tall (5 feet 11 inches), young and appeared to be a man of good breeding. He had no problem in waltzing around Eton and Oxford and would confidently enter premises where members of the lower orders would not consider it their place to tread. Ostrog freely wandered into Eton School and the colleges of Oxford University. He was thought to have received a good education, had good manners and should easily have been capable of obtaining and holding down a decent job had he chosen to do so.

From the prospective of a sexual serial killer, it is

possible that Ostrog was an intelligent man who harboured violent sexual fantasies which stopped him functioning in normal society, resulting in his being constantly in trouble with the law. It is known that many serial killers start out life as petty criminals, breaking and entering into apartments, then as their fantasies overtake them, they then use those skills to break into homes, no longer to steal, but to commit murder. However, Ostrog was not into breaking and entering. He was a confidence trickster, who would steal any valuable possessions that he could lay his hands upon. He was not very successful in his endeavours, having been caught and imprisoned on many occasions.

Ostrog was known to be potentially violent when cornered, and once in 1873 pulled a revolver on the police officers who tried to arrest him for the theft of a few items from Eton School. There is no record of Ostrog actually committing acts of violence against men or women, but on 9 August the Police Gazette had him listed as being wanted for not having reported to the police when on licence following his release from prison. The entry goes on to describe Ostrog as a 'dangerous man'. However, this is most likely to be a warning to fellow police officers that he was the type of man likely to pull a gun on them should they try and arrest him, as opposed to his being a knife welding maniac.

Ostrog appears to have shown up on the Whitechapel police radar because he was released from Surrey Pauper Asylum in March 1888. The investigating officers of the Whitechapel Murder squad having decided that they were dealing with a homicidal manic had requested the names of all recently released mental patients. Ostrog was on one of their lists and so they were duty bound to locate him and then make a decision as to whether or not he might be the Ripper. However, Ostrog was never found so the police were unable to rule him out of their inquiries. Therefore, he would simply have become a sought after suspect simply by being conspicuous by his absence. However, in Ostrog's case, it appears that there was a very good reason why the police were unable to locate him, it appears that he had simply skipped the country and was in France at the time of the murders.

Records show that Ostrog was well known to the French authorities and that he had been arrested and incarcerated on both sides of the English Channel. Ostrog appears to have been in the habit of stealing microscopes and a one Stanislas Lublinski (one of Ostrog's aliases) was arrested in France for the theft of a microscope on 26 July 1888. Lublinski was held in custody until his trial date of 18 November 1888, when he was found guilty and sentenced to two years imprisonment. So in the days before computers and cross border police agencies such as Interpol, Ostrog was safely locked away in the custody of the French Police Force; whilst his absence caused his name to move further and further up the Met Police's list of most wanted Ripper suspects.

Therefore, although perceived as a very dangerous individual by Macnaghten and the Met, Ostrog is the simplest of the three 'prime suspects' to eliminate as he was out of the country for at the time of the murders.

Robert Mann

Robert Mann was a pauper inmate of the Whitechapel workhouse who had charge of the Whitechapel mortuary. The mortuary in Old Montague Street was little more than a converted shed, but was used for the autopsies of Martha Tabram, Mary Ann Nichols and Annie Chapman. Mann is the prime suspect identified by the Ripperologist M.J. Trow in his book 'Jack The Ripper – Quest for a Killer'.

Trow's theory is that Mann, as holder of the keys to the mortuary, would have had access to the surgical instruments used for the dissection of the bodies brought to the building for autopsy. Trow states that Mann was a sexual maniac who skipped the workhouse late at night, went to the mortuary to obtain a surgical knife, prowled around Whitechapel and murdered his victims before returning back to the mortuary to replace the knife and maybe even hide the body parts cut from the victims there. Mann then returned back to the workhouse before the other inmates were woken for their breakfast. Trow writes that Mann was not suspected of perpetrating the crimes by the police or the prostitutes of Whitechapel because they would have been used to seeing him, possibly smeared with blood, in the streets at unusual hours of the day and night.

Even though I am unable to rule him out, if Robert Mann truly was Jack the Ripper, he must have had the luck of the devil. As it was, the Coroner for the South Eastern District of Middlesex Wynne E. Baxter, had little respect for Mann or the mortuary that he held the keys to, and thought that neither had any place in the investigation into the deaths of early Whitechapel Murder victims. It may have been that Baxter sensed that there were going to be further murders and could not see how the any serious investigation could be conducted in a converted shed, maintained by a workhouse inmate. Then again, supposed lack of intelligence and incompetence could have all been part of Mann's scheme of double bluff.

James Maybrick

James Maybrick was a cotton merchant based in Liverpool in Northwest England. He died in May 1889, probably poisoned with arsenic by his American born wife Florence. Florence was found guilty of Maybrick's murder and initially sentenced to death, this being commuted to life imprisonment. Florence was released in 1904 and returned to America, where she died in 1941.

Being a successful married man, working and living in Liverpool, there was no question of Maybrick ever being included in the list of suspects for the London Whitechapel murders back in 1888. However, in 1992 a diary, supposedly written by Maybrick was made public by a former Liverpool scrap metal merchant, Michael Barrett, in which Maybrick is purported to have recorded that he witnessed seeing his wife with her lover in the Whitechapel district of Liverpool, which then led to his going mad and slaughtering the prostitutes in the Whitechapel district of London. Barrett supposedly obtained the diary from a friend, Tony Devereux, in 1991.

Therefore, provided the diary could be dated as being written in 1888-89, you would think that there was a good chance that it might actually be genuine. However, after scientific analysis, it appears that although the binding was of the correct age and that the ink might also have been authentic, some of the written accounts of the murders contain details that were incorrectly reported (possibly intentionally) by the press in 1888. So it is likely that the author of the diary was not actually the Ripper but someone who wrote it basing the details of the murders on old press stories. Also, Barrett has since confessed that the document was a fake. However, the story does not end there and in 1993 a gentleman named Albert Johnson purchased an antique gold watch, only to find that scratched on its inside were the initials of the five Ripper victims, together with the name 'J. Maybrick' and the words 'I am Jack'. Now if a forger had the plan of using the watch to help authenticate the diary, it resulted in the exact opposite effect, with people finding it too hard to believe that the diary and the watch would surface within a year of each other after, after remaining hidden from public view for over 100 years. However, currently neither item has been proved to be a forgery, so unless other items are found or adequate improvements in forensic technology are made, the jury is still out on whether James Maybrick was indeed Jack the Ripper.

Walter Sickert

You will have already seen the name of Walter Sickert, with his son Joseph providing the Ripperologist Stephen Knight with details of the Masonic conspiracy that formed the basis of his book 'Jack The Ripper - The Final Solution'. In his book, Knight wrote that Sir William Gull, Physician-in-Ordinary to Queen Victoria was the Ripper. However, Sickert himself has since been named as a Ripper suspect, by none other than the internationally renowned crime novelist, Patricia Cornwell. Ms Cornwell is reputed to have invested time, money (over 4 million pounds) and effort in a bid to prove that Walter Sickert was Jack the Ripper. She wrote a book 'Portrait of a Killer - Jack The Ripper, Case Closed' based upon the facts that she unearthed about the Whitechapel murders and Sickert's life.

Cornwell's theory was that as a young boy Sickert underwent a series of painful and life threatening operations to treat a fistula (or hole) in his penis. On growing up he supposedly developed a hatred of women, resulting from his being unable to have a normal sex life with them. She added that Sickert used the penname Mr Nobody and unearthed a telegram sent in the name of Jack the Ripper, which was initially signed Mr Nemo, meaning Mr Nobody, in the Latin language. Sickert was known to wander around the Whitechapel area very late at night and liked to dress in costume and disguises. He certainly had an interest in murder and menace, depicting this in many of his drawings and paintings. In addition to this, one of his paintings is entitled 'Jack the Ripper's Bedroom', the room is said to look very much like Sickert's own room when he was living in Camden.

However, as an adult, Sickert married and seems to have had a string of mistresses. Cornwell knew that like all Ripper suspects, she was missing a smoking gun and so she funded DNA testing (far from cheap in 2001-02) of saliva found on the back of stamps affixed to letters sent by Sickert and compared the results against DNA extracted from saliva taken from the back of the stamps affixed to the infamous Jack the Ripper letters. It must be said that interestingly, a match was found on a Ripper letter addressed to a Dr Thomas Horrocks Openshaw, the curator of the pathology museum at the London Hospital. However, the DNA tested was what is known at Mitochondrial DNA, which is far from unique to individuals. So it is possible that Sickert may only have been related somehow to the person that sent the letter in question to Dr Openshaw.

Dr Francis Tumblety

Following an interview by the journalist George R. Sims, Chief Inspector George Littlechild was to write to Sims in September 1913, naming a Canadian quack doctor, Francis Tumblety as the Ripper. Littlechild listed 15 factors which he said indicated that Tumblety was the killer. I can only think that Sims was not much convinced by Littlechild's letter as it took until 1993, when crime historian Stewart P. Evans purchased a batch of Sims' correspondence, for the contents of Littlechild's letter to be made public. Tumblety appears to have been thought a suspect because he was arrested and charged for the offence of gross indecency on 7 November 1888, but was then freed, so was at large when Mary Kelly was murdered early in the morning of 9 November. Tumblety is also reported to have said that he hated women, especially prostitutes and kept a large collection of uteri. In addition to this, there were no more Whitechapel murders attributed to Jack the Ripper following Tumblety's skipping the country for France, before eventually making his way to New York.

There are many reasons why Tumblety could have been the Ripper, however, there is one obvious reason put forward why he could not have been. Tumblety was considered a giant of a man back in the 1880s, standing at least 6 feet tall, with a large head and broad shoulders. In 1888, anyone over 5 feet 10 inches in height would have been considered tall, so a man of Tumblety's huge size would have stood out like a sore thumb. As such, it stretches belief that at a time when all the women out late at night were in fear of their lives, a huge hulking figure could lurk in the shadows without anyone having more than a passing interest in him.

There are a lot more Ripper suspects, but in my opinion, none are credible enough to warrant any further attention.

And there we have it. I have shone the light on Sir Henry Wellcome, a man of greatness who has left a lasting legacy with the Wellcome Trust and Wellcome Foundation PLC. However, he was also a man with an unhealthy interest in surgery and surgical objects, was rumoured to have sadistic tendencies both in and outside of the bedroom and was at breaking point in the summer of 1888.

The Ripper was either a very lucky man or a very clever and cunning man who planned meticulously and covered all his tracks, or more likely a fusion of the two. It is for this reason alone, that Sir Henry Solomon Wellcome FRS deserves to be at least included in the list of prime Ripper suspects.

BIBLIOGRAPHY

Begg, P., Jack The Ripper, The Facts (Portico, 2009)

Birnes, W., and Keppel, R., Signature Killers (Arrow, 1998)

Blegvad, P., Byatt, A.S., Cleary, H, et al, The Phantom Museum and Henry Wellcome's Collection of Medical Curiosities (Profile Books Ltd, 2003)

Chisholm, A., DiGrazia, C-M, Yost, D., The News from Whitechapel, Jack the Ripper in the Daily Telegraph (McFarland & Company, Inc, 2002)

Church, R. and Tansey, E.M., Burroughs Wellcome & Co., Knowledge, Trust, Profit and the Transformation of the British Pharmaceutical Industry, 1880-1940 (Crucible Books, 2007)

Cornwell, P., Portrait of a Killer, Jack The Ripper, Case Closed (Sphere, 2007)

Deer, J., Sir Henry Wellcome – thy will be done (www.briandeer.com, 1993)

Douglas, J., A Criminal Investigative Analysis of Jack The Ripper (Kindle Edition, 2011)

Douglas, J., Burgess, A.W., Ressler. R, & Hartman, C., Criminal Profiling from Crime Scene Analysis (Kindle Edition, 2011)

Douglas, J., Burgess, A.W., Burgess, A.G., & Ressler, R., Crime Classification Manual: A standard system for investigating and classifying violent crime. New York: (Simon and Schuster, 1992)

Eddleston, J.J., Jack the Ripper, an Encyclopaedia (Metro Publishing and imprint of John Blake Publishing Ltd, 2010)

Evans, S.P. and Skinner, K., The Ultimate Jack The Ripper Source Book - An Illustrated Encyclopaedia (Robinson, 2001)

Fitzgerald, M., Ragged London, The Life of London's Poor (The History Press, 2011)

Flannery, J.A. and Smith, K.M., Sir Henry Wellcome, Backwood to Knighthood (Boston Spa Media, 2011)

Harrison, S., Jack The Ripper, The American Connection (Blake Publishing Ltd, 2003)

Hastings, S., The Secret Lives of Somerset Maugham (John Murray (Publishers) An Hachette UK Company, 2010)

James, R.J., Henry Wellcome (Hodder and Stoughton, 1994)

Jones, R., Jack The Ripper - The Casebook (Andre Deutsch, 2008)

Kendell, C., Jack The Ripper – The Theories and the Facts (Amberley Publishing Plc, 2010)

Knight, S., Short, M., The Brotherhood (Kindle Edition, 2010)

Knight, S., Jack The Ripper, The Final Solution (Treasure Press, 1984)

Koven, S., Slumming, Sexual and Social Politics in Victorian London (Princeton University Press, 2004)

Larson, F., An Infinity of Things, How Sir Henry Wellcome Collected the World (Oxford University Press, 2009)

London, J., The People of the Abyss (The Echo Library, 2007)

Lynch, T., Jack the Ripper - The Whitechapel Murderer (Wordsworth Editions Limited, 2008)

Marriott, T. Jack the Ripper, The 21st Century Investigation (John Blake Publishing, 2007)

MacDonald, M., The Threat to Kill (American Journal of Psychiatry, 120 (2):125-130, 1963)

McKnight, G., The Scandal of Syrie Maugham (W.H. Allen, London. A Howard & Wyndham Company, 1980)

Norris, J., Serial Killers - The Growing Menace (Senate Books, 1997)

Douglas, M., Olshaker, J., Mindhunter (Arrow Books, 1997)

Rhodes James, R., Henry Wellcome, (Hodder and Stoughton, 1994)

Ronson, J., The Psychopath Test (Picador, 2012)

Rule, F., The Worst Street in London (Ian Allan Publishing, 2010)

Sugden, P., The Complete History of Jack The Ripper (Robinson, 2002)

Trow, M.J., Jack The Ripper, Quest for a Killer (Wharncliffe True Crime an import of Pen & Sword Books Ltd, 2009)

Turner, H., Henry Wellcome, The Man, His Collection and His Legacy (Heinemann Educational Books Ltd, 1980)

Wagner, G., Barnardo (Eyre & Spottiswoode, 1980)

ABOUT THE AUTHOR

JOSEPH BUSA was educated at Royal Holloway College, University of London, where he took a BSc in Chemistry before going on to study a PGCE in the teaching of science at the University of Southampton. He has had a variety of jobs but hopes that in the writing of books he has found his true vocation in life. He was born and lives in London

Printed in Great Britain
by Amazon